My God Directed Journey

Pauline Heslop

Dedication

This book is dedicated to our children, grandchildren, and future generations to strengthen them with wisdom, courage, and resilience as they seek the path God designs.

About the Author

Dr. Pauline B. Heslop has taken the motto of her alma mater, Ardenne High School in Jamaica, West Indies: *"Deo Duce Quaere Optima"* as her inspiration to seek the best with God as her guide. Her outstanding personal and professional accomplishments attest to her success in following that admonition.

The author graduated cum laude with a B.S. in chemistry from Hunter College in New York and began her medical career after obtaining an M.D. degree from Downstate Medical College. Dr. Heslop's extensive and varied experience has taken her to several hospitals in New York. She completed her residency at Metropolitan Hospital and Westchester County Medical Center and a clerkship at Montefiore Hospital. She has also served in the Emergency Room at Metropolitan Hospital.

Dr. Heslop maintained a private practice with admitting privileges at Montefiore Hospital and voluntary attending privileges at both Montefiore Hospital and Jacobi Hospital of the North Bronx Healthcare Network for over twenty years.

After becoming involved in Pediatrics, Dr. Heslop recognized her passion for working with young people. For over twenty-three years, she has served as the Medical Director of Covenant House, the nation's largest Adolescent care agency serving at-risk youth in New York. Her knowledge, commitment, and dedication to the needs of disenfranchised and homeless youth have equipped her to guide the Health Services Department of Covenant House in fulfilling its mission.

Under the author's leadership, the medical services provided by Covenant House have been strengthened, including, among other things, the improvement of the Medicaid eligibility program and the introduction of ophthalmologic and on-site dental screenings. In addition, the excellent quality of client care has earned Dr. Heslop and her team a patient satisfaction rating above 90%, with an average of over 95% of clients expressing their willingness to continue receiving healthcare at that facility.

The author's humanitarianism and concern for youth are motivated and guided by her love and commitment to the Lord. So, her role as Physician and Medical Director was not simply a job. It was an assignment from the Lord God Almighty. This assignment was extended to counseling young people at the Spofford Juvenile Detention Center in the Bronx. She has also served as chairperson of several ministries of the Bronx Baptist Church. Her call to the ministry and her natural inclination in this area of service has been academically enhanced by her attainment of a Master of Divinity degree with an emphasis on counseling from Alliance Theological Seminary in 2007.

Dr. Heslop is the daughter of the late Sylvan and Mildred Small. She is married to Rupert Heslop, and they are the parents of three children. She is also a mother-in-law and incredibly proud to be a grandmother of seven beautiful children. Reverend Dr. Heslop's greatest desire and mission is to know that lives are transformed through God's grace and mercy.

Prologue

My Dear Children and Friends,

As you read my letters and journal entries, I know they will empower you to walk boldly into your purpose. This written record of my experiences will assist you and the future generations on their upcoming journey. I intentionally prepared my memoir to strengthen you with the knowledge of who you are; for our Sovereign, Uncreated, Almighty, All-Knowing, All Seeing, Powerful Creator God has purposely created and gifted us. He has uniquely designed each person to have a loving relationship with Him. However, the development and maintenance of that relationship are the keys to our eternal existence.

The goal is to encourage you to become deeply acquainted with God and prove that it's possible to draw near Him and see Him as an ever-present help in trouble. After reading, you will see that obedience to God's will can be experienced as the key to true and lasting peace, especially in seasons when you come upon what seems like unconquerable mountains.

Affirmations

Many people deserve affirmations.

I want to acknowledge and applaud everyone who has impacted my life. Some have done so positively and others negatively, but you helped me become the best I could be. So today, I'd like to thank those who have positively impacted my life and let you know that your presence and prayers have been highly beneficial.

First, I am incredibly grateful to my late, very pious grandmother Wilhelmina Duncan, my parents, my powerfully praying mother, Mildred Small, a daughter of the Bennett Duncan clan, and my family-oriented father, Sylvan Small. Next, I must applaud my husband, Rupert Heslop, who has stood with me since we became acquainted and linked by God's grace. Finally, much appreciation is due to my sisters, the late Melrose Johnson, the bold Floona Small Seville, Adlin Small Benjamin, Lana, and Sharon Small. In addition, my late brothers Nelton and Fitzroy Small, nieces Delrose Bryan and Charlene Foulkes, and our family friend Jean Fagan and other family members have all uniquely provided me support.

Last but not least, I must give love and much gratitude to my supportive children, Wayne Heslop,

Tisha Williams, and Richard Heslop; my son-in-law and Pastor, The Rev. Frank I. Williams; my daughter-in-law, Erynn Heslop, and my grandchildren Brielle, Timothy, Tiffany, Trinity, Thomas, Raygen, Richard Junior, and my spiritual children, grandchildren, and many other supportive family members and friends.

My thanks should also go to my dedicated and highly appreciated prayer partners - Rhona, Doxie, Vivienne, and the late sisters Hermine Williams and Monica White. I'd also like to acknowledge Renee, who has often morally supported me. Thanks to Minister Hyacinth Sang, sister Griffiths, and Minister Dr. Edna Barnett from other ministries for your prayerful consistency. In addition, I must take time to thank my editors and their support team.

Contents

Chapter 1: God's Unique/Personalized Manner of Communicating with Me

"My son, if you receive my words and treasure up my commandments with you, making your ear attentive to wisdom and inclining your heart to understand; yes, if you call out for insight and raise your voice for understanding if you seek it like silver and search for it as for hidden treasures, then you will understand the fear of the Lord and find the knowledge of God."

(Proverbs 2:1-5)

God is omnipresent and omniscient; He is covert yet seen; He is beyond the skies and still close to us. He communicates to us in so many unique ways, sometimes through His creation, other times through divine intervention, but all the time through His word. He chooses how and when to reveal Himself to people.

There is no fixed pattern regarding how God speaks or delivers; for some, the Bible could be the source of communication; for others, it's the Bible coupled with dreams, visions, trusted advisors, and His spiritual presence. I have experienced God's contact through divine interventions that have enlightened me throughout my life. This is so valuable that I must pass on my insights on God's communication to my children and all the generations to come.

I thank God for His grace and mercy and the Holy Spirit's divine intervention in awakening and using me. It was only recently that I had a brief reflection on how God speaks to us. It was a pointed reminder because my understanding and response to His way of speaking have allowed me to participate in God's work of deliverance for many.

Individuals in my family and other families have experienced this act of release. God is a splendid protector equipped to destroy negativity, especially evil forces surrounding a person. He is our protector when we are unaware and our guide when we lack understanding.

People often say, *"God covers fools and babies."* It is not said to offend anyone, as the meaning implies that you are not equipped to care for or protect yourself if viewed as a baby. But, on the contrary, be assured that God will ultimately safeguard and protect those who are helpless and hopeless, especially when there is no protective caregiver.

Similarly, a fool is someone who, despite obvious proven facts, chooses to do the very opposite of that which is seen and known to be beneficial. Finally, fools may also be categorized as individuals who deliberately cover their eyes and stop their ears when others with a special gift of discernment try to caution them to listen and act in a manner that will be protective.

God reveals the truth to us in mysterious ways. In my case, I have found my relationship with God through His word and prayers. My first prominent remembrance of a divine intervention relates to my youngest son. I was amazed when I realized God had communicated His insights through worship. The experience was somewhat surreal because when it happened, I could not stop praying and praising for a while.

My first experience of communication was on a fine Wednesday afternoon. I returned early from work and expected my son to arrive home from school. And as he came, I was prompted to call him for prayer.

So, I found myself saying, *"Come in here, son. I need to pray for you. Come and kneel by my bed."*

He did so willingly, and this was when the intervention event transpired.

As soon as we began to pray, I for him and he in submission before God – my spiritual eyes were opened. It was pretty surprising because it was very unusual to me. I could see myself pulling away from his body energy that I can only describe as dirty, tattered, tangled-up cords oozing from his mouth. I realized this was God's communication with me at this particular moment.

To this day, I don't know how such energy got into him, but I thank God for His Divine Awakening of my

Spirit to see and obey His directives. However, I did not stop praying for a while, as I did not want the communication to end.

Before this incident, I had a somewhat similar experience. It is essential to mention that during another of my prayers, I, too, had to be spiritually detoxed. While praying, I saw myself pulling tangled-up messy cords from my mouth. I will share later what I believe this was related to, but I want to focus on how the Holy Spirit has allowed me to discern and pray for others.

The second significant experience brought to light how the mouth of doubt, resentment, and fear of a person can manifest in other people's lives. The encounter I experienced happened just when my daughter was promoted to another class by the grace of God. Unfortunately, I couldn't attend the parent-teacher meeting, but my mom accompanied my daughter.

In that school, it was common practice for teachers to post their students' names, grades, and performances on a poster board. My daughter was listed amongst those on the honor roll. However, my mom shared that a woman present spoke words that evoked a bit of trepidation.

Mom said she was disturbed not because of the words spoken, as this woman belonged to the house of the Living God but especially by how her words were spoken.

The following words came from her lips: *"Wow, are you on the honor roll again?"*

But, according to Mom, the words were said with a hint of cynicism and dread. As far as I can recall, that was the last time my daughter achieved that status of honors in elementary school.

In addition, my daughter was part of a speakers group organized for young people. Again, like all the other children, we entrusted her to the hands of capable leaders. It was common practice for children to be given under very trusted leadership. We did so because I used to be scheduled for work on Saturdays, and her Father, my husband, was also unable to take the trip. But, this time, an unseen watchman was on that trip. He was unknown to the group.

In retrospect, I can only say he was placed there by God as a source of communication. When the session ended, he contacted my husband. He was very excited and, at the same time, showed much concern.

He said, *"Man! I don't know what happened in that place, but your daughter should have won that tournament. Something is not right!"* He added, *"They gave the award to someone who did well, but your daughter's speech brought the audience to tears. She deserved the award. I don't understand why she was not given the winning prize."*

Two other young persons echoed his statement, adding that they wished we would have been there.

Our daughter was upset about not winning, but little did she know that the audience recognized her. I encouraged her not to worry as God had allowed her to accomplish what He sent her there to do. She settled with that, and I can only say thanks to God for His instructive words penned by the Prophet Jeremiah:

"For I know the plans I have for you," declares the Lord. "Plans to prosper you and not to harm you, plans to give you hope and a future."

(Jeremiah 29:11).

This is where I learned that God's plan for His children could not be thwarted. Therefore, He continued to order my steps and those of my daughter so that I would become more attuned and obedient to His voice. Some of the other phases of my life guided by Him are mentioned in this chapter to assist you in understanding the ways and means God uses to communicate and guide us all.

God has spoken to me several times at different stages of my life. I would get these dreams and visions that are beneficial not only for me but for many others. While sitting at my dining table in the home,

God had *"directed us to purchase,"* the Holy Spirit downloaded a picture of my nephew to my Spirit. I immediately got up from the table and went to the door. As I opened the door, the same nephew was walking past my house, to my amazement. They lived a couple of blocks away from my home.

I remember very emphatically saying these unrehearsed words to him, *"Don't go into that car again! If you get in that car, something serious will happen."*

Unfortunately, this young man did not listen to me, and in a matter of some hours or a day later when I was told he had an accident while driving in a car with his friend. The vehicle was severely damaged, and his mother was found liable for the damage.

Here are two other incidents that I must mention; they involve my husband. I can recall being spontaneously aroused. It was dark and might have been nighttime or probably the wee hours of the morning, but we were both awakened simultaneously. He had a dream, and I envisioned someone breaking into our son's car. We both discussed it and decided to check on our son. We both went to the window and looked out toward the street.

To our disbelief, someone stood over our son's vehicle with a light shining into the front window as if he was searching for something. As we turned on our bedroom light, that person turned off their light and vanished. It was undoubtedly God that had communicated to us so that we could avoid that break-in.

After this incident and others, my belief in God grew more potent than ever. I became fully aware that protecting and alerting us in many ways to turn things in our favor and goodwill is God's doing.

"He who dwells in the shelter of the Highest will abide in the shadow of the Almighty. I will say to the Lord, my refuge and fortress, my God, whom I trust; for he will deliver you from the snare of the fowler and the deadly pestilence. He will cover you with his pinions, and under his wings, you will find refuge; his faithfulness is a shield and buckler. You will not fear the terror of the night nor the arrow that flies by day..."

-(Psalm 91:1-16)

Similarly, here's another situation I found genuinely unique. I was on call in the Pediatric Nursery at Metropolitan Hospital. It was time for my break, and I needed to have dinner, so I began thinking about what I would have as a meal. I desired to have shrimp, broccoli, and baked potato. However, my thoughts and actions were soon interrupted by the on-call operator.

"Dr. Heslop, a gentleman is here to see you," they told me.

I went to the lobby, and to my amazement, my husband stood there with a covered tray. He had brought me dinner, but the timing revealed that God is Spectacular and Magnificent. My prayer was lifted just before my dinner break. I needed a meal, but God had already alerted my husband to prepare the desired meal even before I thought of it. I don't recall verbalizing the details of the desired meal, but they were in my thoughts and were my heart's desires.

When I looked at the meal, I could only say, "God, You genuinely care for me, for us. You care so deeply and so precisely."

Of course, I was pregnant, and it was a delicious meal, but the tastiest delights were the lessons learned from God's response.

This reminded me of when the Prophet Isaiah said,

"Before they call, I will answer, and while they are still speaking (about their needs), I will hear."

(Isaiah 65:24)

These lessons, as well as many other incidents, were preparation for something that would make a difference between life and death for someone very dear to my heart.

I am writing this book to empower readers to walk boldly toward their purpose, which God has uniquely gifted them. In addition, this book is intended to guide the reader in identifying the key to lasting peace and how they can face increased pressures or unconquerable obstacles. I believe that God communicates to us at every step of our lives. Therefore, we must be vigilant and knowledgeable enough to recognize the signs and be grateful for the guidance.

My daughter and sons went away to college. I did not worry much because I had trusted in their lessons, their upbringing under the banner of God, and their acceptance of the Lord Jesus Christ as the Savior of their life. I believed that it would be enough to keep them protected. However, on my part, I have learned the hard way that while God's hand is upon you, there come times when you must dig deep to protect your family and solidify your trust in the Lord.

I thank God for His covering and protective wisdom, His messengers, and the strength He has given me to do my part in protecting. He is the designer and creator of all good things, and I firmly believe He has given us the best path to find His plans. And repeatedly, I have been shown through His communication that my beliefs are legitimate.

I have been guided and taught by Him throughout my life. However, these were not the only times I felt a strong relationship with God. There have been several incidents where I had the epiphany that God is looking at us and communicating His messages through visions, dreams, and circumstances.

Chapter 2: The Calling and Preparation for My Life's Work

"God is our refuge and strength, a present help in trouble. Bible verses about relying on God's strength when we look to God, he will give us the strength we need to carry us through the dark times."

— (Psalm 46:1)

The most beautiful part of my journey has been my calling and preparation for my life's work. To begin with, I got a scholarship at the very young age of eleven. Scholarships are often given out earlier in the English domain. I was awarded a scholarship after completing the high school entrance examination in Kingston, Jamaica, West Indies. This scholarship opened my eyes to a whole different environment. It was a beautiful school with an aesthetic view. The school's campus was lined with trees and grass. I can still visualize a circle of wooden benches surrounded by several trees. Students would sit and chat privately during the breaks on the benches at the base of the trees.

My scholarship was a great help because my family of eight was not among the most highly privileged. So, the scholarship covered all my school necessities, from books to lunches and tuition. Because of my scholarship, my Father did not have to worry about anything. He invested all the money that belonged to me and gave it to me when needed.

Passion for Becoming a Medical Doctor

At school, one very caring teacher would always guide us in our daily activities. I was very much fascinated with science. And luckily, I had a friend with the same level of interest as me. We used to talk about our passions and dreams, what we would do in the future, and what would happen. At that time, she and I were the only ones in our class who wanted to pursue medicine as a career path.

My interest in medicine was due to my curiosity about the human body. The pivotal part of school was attending chemistry, biology, physics, and even math classes. I loved science, and along with my friend, so I did well in these subjects.

I was passionate about pursuing medicine to such an extent that while taking my exams, I only thought about my grades at the end of the year. I have had this passion for doing well in my academics my entire life. I believe this happened because God had chosen this path for me. He wanted me to pursue medicine, but I barely understood that then. The only thing I knew was that I was a person who loved to read and would read any book at any given moment.

I have always been grateful for what I have been blessed with. However, one day there was a book that

I desperately needed. I remember our teacher bringing the books to school; one was left behind. It was just lying on the table, and as I particularly like books, I thought to bring it home. I did not know if it belonged to me, but I needed this book.

When I returned home, my mother was unhappy with what I did. She demanded that I take the book back to school because it did not belong to me as it did not have my name on it and was not given to me; that was when I learned how important honesty is. Ever since then, I have been living with this trait of openness within me by the grace of God.

Pursuing medicine has always been my ambition. I dreamed about becoming a doctor and used to love to discuss my future with my friend. At that time, my sister's nursing profession enticed me. I read her books and felt excited as I looked at the pictures. I was a curious child and longed to know exactly how and why the human body functioned the way it did.

This passion was further enhanced as I went to the hospital and saw a young male doctor—with a stethoscope around his neck, a writing pad, and a pen in his hand. I looked at him captivated; as he moved from patient to patient, he journaled and directed the staff of the day's proceedings. He appeared to be equipped and was obviously in charge. Later, I found out that he and others were on medical rounds.

As I looked at him and saw how he expressed leadership skills and how others looked avidly at him and accepted his directives, I knew then that I was heading in the right direction. To my surprise, when my sister was choking while we were alone, I knew exactly what to do; later, I was supernaturally advised of the condition of several patients before they came to see me at the hospital. Finally, the Lord had placed within me a desire to enter this field, to care for others healthily. There and then, He also instilled within me the desire to value excellence.

"Whatever your hand finds to do, do it with all your might, for in the realm of the dead, where you are going, there is neither working nor planning nor knowledge or wisdom."

– (Ecclesiastes 9:10)

Desire to Excel

As I sit here recapping the story of my life, I can now clearly comprehend why I desire to know not only my grades but how I performed in each subject in high school. It was indeed God who had planted within me a desire for excellence. All the other students called me *"Miss Detail"* because of my longing to always aim for perfection. In high school, I received honors in Sciences, Latin, and Math and was encouraged to pursue the university application process.

However, at that time, my sister relocated from England to the U.S.A. after completing her nursing course and degree. She called me to live with her, and I believe this was all a part of God's plan. God promises to us that He will make room for our giftedness. Precisely, that is what He did for me, as He allowed my sister to have me come to the United States to live with her.

In the beginning, there was some amount of uncertainty as to what my path would be. Still, that uncertainty was quickly erased because I entered Hunter College, where I began studying the sciences with chemistry as my primary area and math as my minor.

I worked hard and graduated with a cum laude degree. However, during the process, there were some experiences that I will never forget. I did not understand the events that occurred then. And I used to be often hurt at that moment. But looking back at each experience, I can see why these experiences are essential to guide others, including my biological and spiritual children and grandchildren. I see how it will help them find and chart their God-given course despite all the prejudice and attacks from others.

God has created a path affirming and solidifying that path for each individual. He has supernaturally equipped us with the Spirit of excellence for a specific purpose and a uniquely designed slot. God is the master designer who cannot and does not make garbage. Instead, He has wonderfully and fearfully made each of us in His likeness.

As the saying goes, ' *God, The Blessed Three in One, cares for us more than we can comprehend.* '

It took me a while to hold on to the depth of this truth. But finally, when I did, I understood that all the other discordant voices have only attempted to dictate otherwise.

Meeting My Husband: Part of God's Plan

My sister moved to the U.S. to pursue her nursing career and needed company. Unfortunately, my mother could not go because she needed to care for my grandmother. So, I joined my sister after I graduated from high school. The goal was to accompany my sister while pursuing my education. In the interim, I got a job at Mays department store.

My job was to manage the elevators up and down manually. A guy was working there part-time in the stock room. He showed interest in me and wanted to take me out for lunch. I believed that building this kind of relationship would not be suitable for my studies, and I did not want to do this because my mind was utterly bent on school. I tried to focus on my studies. So, I told him he did not need to buy me lunch because I had money and could purchase my food on my own. But he liked me and continued to try to win my heart. And eventually, he won.

My husband was in automotive school, and I was in college when we decided to get married. My sister was very concerned about me getting married this early and not waiting until the end of my degree. My brother-in-law did not favor this initially, as he wanted me to marry someone he had in mind.

However, they blessed me after seeing how happy I was with him. So, the wedding happened at the Church we attended. Although it rained heavily that day, it was a beautiful Church ceremony. My brother-in-law was my giveaway father because my parents could not participate in the wedding. I viewed the rain as a cleansing blessing, for soon after the rain, the sun came shining through. The ceremony was followed by a reception at my sister's home; they had a lovely house in Queens. Everyone was quite happy; my cousins made the cake, and my aunt was beside me throughout the preparation.

We are blessed with three children. I had the first one in college and the second when I entered medical school; the last one was given to us by God during my residency. It is challenging to handle marriage and three children with a full-time career. Still, I was blessed that it all worked out eventually. I know it was God's grace that made it all happen smoothly.

On the other hand, my husband helped me a lot; I did not have to go to the supermarket for the longest time because he was the one shopping. There were times when I was doing the rotations, and I would go home late in the evening to be with them just for a few hours. He would not let me worry about the children or home.

My husband took care of everything, even getting the children to school. It would not have been possible to pull all of this together if it were not for him. He has played a significant role in my life, making it much lighter. So much so that I remember one lady in the Church coming up to me and saying she could not even believe it. Nobody knew that I was in medical school. No one learned what I was studying until I graduated.

In one of my classes, I had the most outstanding experience because I remember the voice that spoke for it impacted my physics in calculus class. I found that class fascinating, and I did well. It was indeed part of God's plans that I met my husband. I continued my studies as a married student with a child in college. It seemed effortless as I viewed my walk-in step with what I now realize as God's plan. Although, at times, many of my former actions seem so tricky. I was taking that class when my husband told me he had a specific assignment to be addressed in Manhattan. He needed my help and asked me to do that leg of the journey for him.

We both assumed it would be easy to manage since the assignment was in mid-Manhattan near Hunter College. So, I left earlier that morning, went to the office location, and accomplished the task, only to realize that I had limited time to get uptown for my scheduled class examination.

As I walked up Park Avenue, I decided to hail a cab, but to my amazement, no taxi stopped for me. So, I ran. I walked alternately, looking out, hoping one would respond to my signal, but none stopped. So, I entered the class after test papers were handed out and students were glued to their exam papers. I was a ball of nerves, and I apologized for being late. Then, I took the test papers and sat down.

Despite studying for several days for this test, nothing came to mind as I glanced at the exam questions. All I could do was cry out for help from God; I repeatedly said, *"God help me."* Finally, the voice spoke, and I was directed to start at the bottom, which I did. That was just the beginning of great things. Soon after completing that question, my memory bank opened, and I felt confident. I could complete the examination with spare time to review my answers. Surprisingly, I left the session early because of the timely completion. Thanks be to God, who is *a very present help in trouble. (Psalm 46:1)*

The following week, I was greeted with excellent news. My final grade was A+. According to the test remarks, every answer was correct, including the bonus answers. I continued college and graduated with honors in chemistry.

My Medical School Application

Despite my academic achievement, I was alarmed when I spoke to my preceptor about the next steps of my journey, namely, my medical school application. My assigned preceptor was the same teacher who had just recently finalized my grade, with an honors designation in physics with calculus. My conversation with my teacher amazed me when I met with him per schedule. First, he asked what I wanted to do, to which I said I wanted to become a doctor.

His response was, *"Why don't you become a teacher?"*

I felt a bit disappointed and probably hurt at first. I did not know what to say, but after pausing briefly, I opened my mouth, and these words came out, *"May I ask you a question."*

To this, he replied, *"Sure."*

I quickly responded, *"You wanted to be a teacher, didn't you? However, I have wanted to be a doctor since I was seven years old, and with or without you, I will make that happen."*

This was so unlike me; I thought to myself, wow! *Where did that come from?* I was scared and upset, thinking I had probably shattered my dreams and would not get the evaluation I needed to get into medical school.

However, God has mysterious ways to clear your path toward your goal. After a brief period, I was called to the office and handed an envelope. I was surprised to see that this was the best recommendation that I had received for my medical school application. I was so content that I kept a copy I treasured for many years. However, in relocating, I might have displaced it. I can't recall that teacher's name anymore. Still, my prayer is for the blessings of God Almighty to rest upon him and his family. I know that he has been put in God's care.

"God rewards honest and faithful people, especially those who care for babies, the needy, and the poor."

— (Psalm 41:1-3)

I proceeded with the submission of my applications to two or three medical schools. Two universities still stand out for several reasons. The first interview that I was called to was at Howard University. I applied there because it was known to be a prestigious Black University. I had great chances with my grades, honors on my college certificate, and those wonderful letters of recommendation.

However, there was an unseen problem, and I did not anticipate their response. After the interview, I was told straight-up to my face without any equivocation that because I went to a predominantly White college, I would not be able to settle well at a Black University.

I was surprised because I genuinely thought to God that if I thrived anywhere, it would be in such a University amongst people like me. I understand that maybe they perceived that I considered myself better than they are. Still, they were so blatantly wrong to prejudge me. My following interview was at Downstate Medical Center, which went well.

The University had predominantly Jewish students at that time. I later found out that only twenty ("*minority*") African-American students were in my class. Nevertheless, I learned valuable lessons I hope the younger generation can glean.

The first lesson is that you often face preconceived notions that you are not as good as you might be despite God's design. In my predominantly Jewish class, no one expected me to do as well as I did. I recall doing a biochemistry exam for which I had worked hard. That is the thing about me; I spent much time ensuring I had completed all the assignments in preparation for an exam. The exam was challenging, but I finished it within the given time.

When the exam review came, I noticed that two questions needed to be graded correctly. After distributing the graded exam sheets, I remember that the teacher had gone over the questions in class and revealed the correct answers. So, of course, I took my paper in and asked for a review because it needed to be graded correctly.

He responded, *"You may think you're the brightest in this class, but you're not."*

My question had nothing to do with his answer – a comparative statement. This showed where the heart of humanity resides. My question was not a comparative analysis of my ability, nor was this an examination to determine my capacities.

I responded, *"Professor, if I had erred in answering the questions and needed those points to have a passing grade, you wouldn't have given it to me, right? Now that I have earned those points, I'm asking you to make the necessary adjustments."*

Unfortunately, he did not make the adjustments.

This lesson should have equipped me for the subsequent encounter. Still, the following example will reveal how difficult it is to acquire the cunning craftiness of humanity and how difficult it is to understand how they are when you are taught to walk with the Lord and have learned only fairness and equity.

That being said, on another day, just before the professor came into class, I was approached by a student who wanted to know what I had studied for the course; I was excited to share, without realizing that he only wanted to pick my brain. So *"I began to rattle off everything I had gleaned from my studies."* It was shocking to hear my Caucasian classmate relaying what I had shared with him earlier, even though he told me he did not study as he was having fun. I could not believe my ears.

Surgical Rotations at Brooklyn Hospital

Even after all that, I did not learn my lesson. On the contrary, the upcoming one was a bit more painful and heartbreaking since the dagger came *"from my familiar friend,"* if she could be considered one.

During our elective year at Downstate, I and a few others from my class were assigned to a surgical rotation. Transportation was difficult since it was across town, from Downstate Medical College to Brooklyn Hospital, and I had to either take a taxi or drive. To make it easier, my husband and I shared our only car.

I used to travel by train, but I used the car on the days assigned for the surgical rotations. We lived in the Bronx, and our noted experience was that a train commute was not always the easiest way to get to classes at Downstate or Brooklyn. So, that was why I was given the car.

I became friends with a young woman. We developed a cordial relationship; she began traveling with me back and forth. At the end of our daily sessions, I often took a detour to drop her off at Downstate even if, the truth be told, I did not have to go in that direction. We developed what I thought was a good relationship, so I invited her to my particular space, a group, and a fellowship event at the Church that was meaningful to me. I expected her from our communications, but she did not show up.

During our conversations, she shared with me that she and her team had some past examinations they used to prepare for the upcoming board examinations. She said she would share them with me when we returned to campus. However, upon our return, she acted as if I did not exist at the close of the rotation. She was with others in the hallway on campus when I tried to get her attention, but she looked directly at me as if I were invisible. After a few attempts with my quiet demeanor, I soon realized it was her avoidance strategy.

Later on, when I thought about it, I concluded that I was possibly viewed as a threat for no reason except because I was conscientious and well-learned.

Moreover, she no longer needed my car, as the rotation was over. Of course, this behavior from people with whom you have spent most of your waking hours and have done nothing but extend a hand of kindness is very painful. However, I want the readers to know that if you are on the right path of God, no one can destroy you. Weapons will form, but they will not prosper. They have limited power. That is to say; by God's grace and the diligence that He gave me to study, I could come through those exams with flying colors without assistance from those past exam papers.

I learned to maintain my trust in God the hard way, and I do not want children to go through that same pain if possible. The purpose of sharing my experiences is to teach children to be polite with each other and stay vigilant around everyone.

"The way of the wicked is an abomination unto the LORD: but he loves him who follows after righteousness."

– (Proverbs 15:9)

My Residency

After my medical school ended, I started my residency program at Metropolitan Hospital. It is often said that a City Hospital is the best place to be trained, and I can affirm that now. I acquired many great medical/clinical lessons and skills at

Metropolitan, where I experienced one of my greatest hurts. Our great God is, however, a healer and restorer if we are only willing to accept His healing.

While on one of my rotations, I can picture the ward even now. It was a jam-packed evening. I was on a thirty-six-hour call and had previously spent many days/hours preparing for an upcoming grand rounds presentation at the end of the residency program at a Metropolitan Hospital. Since I spent most of my time there, I carried the paper I had finished with me, and I am curious to know how the chief resident on call got wind of it.

We always left our bags with everything unlocked.

Finally, one day she came up to me after a busy overnight shift and, as if she cared, said, *"You must be exhausted. Why don't you let somebody else read your document?"*

I was very timid, so when confronted by a supervisor with something that did not seem wrong, somehow, I agreed, and the next thing I knew, she allowed a Latino woman to present my work as if it was her own.

My Naiveté toward People

The fraudulent event during my residency taught me my naiveté toward people. I foolishly hoped this lady presenting my work would give me my due credit for the job. But little did I know she was stepping in and replacing me.

I never imagined that this would ever happen to me. So, I sat there quietly and heard word by word, my presentation being read by another person. I waited to hear my name called, but it did not happen. So, instead, I sat there listening to the professor saying, excellent work and everybody giving accolades to the girl reading my presentation. It was a very heart-wrenching experience; I could not move for a moment; I just sat there weeping; nobody came or asked me why I was crying. It was as if I was invisible.

I did not say a word to anyone. All I did when everybody left was get up, wash my face, and return to work but with a heavy burden on my heart. I had somehow buried this pain in me for a long time. As I began to write this book, many displeasing feelings and unanswered questions were returning. Still, our merciful God has lightened the load and revealed how I should use this experience to help myself and others.

All that is left for me to say is that you never know how wicked one person can be to another. To my dismay, my work was presented exactly as it was written. I sat there and heard my report being relayed by another voice. I sat there listening to the accolades given to the person behind that voice and not to me, who worked diligently, sacrificing my evenings, family time, and many other essential things. I was first frozen, then I became numb. I still cannot fathom why I did not report the matter. I know that I cannot personally recoup these losses. After numerous years it still boggles my mind as I relay the story.

However, I thank God for His presence and guiding hand in and over my life because He has helped me to take firm steps in helping others. In retrospect, I pray that I have enough time and wisdom to help others to avoid those pitfalls. Of course, I cannot do so alone, but by God's grace and the Spirit of forgiveness, I can help make life's journey less treacherous for others. The great singer Mahalia Jackson said it this way.

If I can help somebody as I travel along

If I can help somebody with a word or song

If I can help somebody from doing wrong

No, my living shall not be in vain

My prayer, deeds, and encouragement to all of us are that we should plan to live our God-given lives so that our life's journey will not be in vain.

Chapter 3: Lessons from God's Hand

"So do not fear, for I am with you; do not be dismayed, for I am your God. I will strengthen and help you; I will uphold you with my righteous right hand."

- Isaiah 41:10

We might not be able to see it sometimes, but God helps humanity in many ways. Yet, we often fail to notice the little occurrences in our daily lives that denote He is trying to help us. I firmly believe that God's encounters are designed not only for the individual who experiences them but also for those around them. I can recall several such meetings, but the one that stands out right now, as of this writing, is the one that occurred when I was driving up the highway for a scheduled appointment.

As I traveled, the highway seemed so clogged; every move I made was unfruitful. The traffic was jammed, so I could not get through or move to another lane. It was a bit perplexing, and I was stressed because I had committed to assisting others with my prayer and presence. My word and commitment to worship were significant to me.

I only commit if I know I can fulfill it. So, as I continued my journey, it became even more perplexing. I tried looking for an exit point or a way out of the congested highway. After a long and challenging time, I finally found a way and sneaked through it. I sighed in relief and thought to myself, indeed, I would now get to my designated location, but the hindrances continued because the streets were quite jam-packed, and I could not get to the scheduled area. In addition, I became flustered, uncertain of the exact address, and was lost at one point. So, I called and told the individuals I was running late and needed to confirm the address.

The response was, *"Don't worry about it. Since it's so late, we will just come to the Church meeting."*

It was two-pronged in that it was an experience of relief when the situation ended, but it was bewilderment upon reflection on the incident. However, after some time, when I reflected on this incident, I realized that God did not want me to be a part of that session. At that point, I couldn't understand why, but the answers came much later. Two couples were to gather there for prayer about their potential union. My role was to pray for them, and I truly desired to do so, but God had other plans unknown to all involved. That is to say, one of the unions was not a part of God's plan, but none of us knew that then.

I can now talk about it, but at that point, I was very frustrated because no matter what I did, my journey was blocked by many obstacles. I tried everything I could, but nothing worked. I could do absolutely nothing to change the outcome. The outcomes revealed that one of the couples would enter into matrimony later, and the other decided not to marry. This was God's project, and He made ways for them to realize His plan by blocking my way. That is to say, God had closed the door and stopped me from going there to support what He had not ordained.

"The LORD directs the steps of the Godly. He delights in every detail of their lives. Therefore, though they stumble, they will never fall, for the LORD holds them by the hand."

- Psalm 37:23

Through the encounters experienced in my life, I am confident that the lessons from God have always been there in front of me. His guidance made me realize and notice those signs and speeches. I have learned that no harm can penetrate when God has a hand on His children. This writing provides indicators to find the true path He has chosen for us. And if we listen well, we will always be guided.

Another time, I got a call from the receptionist at my small neighborhood office. She stated that a young man had come to see me and wondered when I would come to the office. I responded that I was on the highway and would be there shortly. It was evening hours, and I was going from the clinic in Manhattan to my small office in the Bronx. As I was driving, the

Holy Spirit prompted me to move out of that lane. I was in the right lane but didn't move. The inner prompting came again and again.

The inner voice kept coming; *Move over! Move Over!* The directive was emphasized with a pause between the two words, but I did not heed the warning. Unfortunately, as I continued in the same lane, I felt a big bang on the roof of my car; thinking and feeling that the top was about to cave in on my head, I ducked down to protect my head. Praise be to God; it didn't happen. I thought it would hit me because the sound was highly deafening. However, because of His Mercy and His protective hand, there was no damage to the car, and above all, I was fine.

The Lord was preparing me to listen and know His voice. He is an Extraordinary Sovereign Being whose hand is divinely protective; nothing is ever wasted under His protection.

"All things work together for good to them that love God, to them who are the called according to His purpose."

(Romans 8:28)

These incidents made me value His signs and understand His voice more clearly. They also prepared me for many other issues that would be revealed later. However, these two incidents were significant occurrences for me. It was just so uncanny. I know it has to be the hand of God, which is protective and merciful. He protects us even when we ignore the signs and voices. While these two incidents were essential and very important to me, they were not the only ones through which He showed me how deeply protective He is.

Knowing someone was waiting, I continued to drive and tried my best to get there, but again I was blocked at every turn. Finally, when I got to the office, my receptionist said she was very fearful because the young man had been there asking about me thrice. She further relayed that there was an eerie feeling about his presence. It was a feeling that she wasn't very safe in his company. For her, it wasn't very comforting. I thought about it and realized that that young man possibly meant harm to me and not good, which is why God had allowed a delay on my journey. To this day, I am not sure what that was all about.

Soon after that (Hallelujah God), someone cooperated and strategized with the enemy to make me sick at work. Brothers and sisters in Christ, I had suffered a severe attack. When it first happened, I didn't realize its spiritual nature. But in the wee hours, I developed severe stomach pains and vomiting. The Holy Spirit usually awakened me at 5 AM. I would go into the bathroom and pray quietly to avoid disturbing anyone.

My prayers were often in tongues (the heavenly language mentioned earlier). This is because God had previously supernaturally equipped me by baptizing me with the Holy Spirit and the gifts of tongues. I subsequently often prayed for many. However, after a while, I suddenly stopped. And I cannot explain the reason for stopping.

Maybe it was a feeling of fatigue or the enemy blocking my participation in God's work. Nevertheless, on that particular day, my husband and mother diligently helped to alleviate that episode of pain and vomiting.

However, when I returned to work the next week, I continued to do things as usual. At lunchtime, I again got my food from the refrigerator, warmed it, and quickly ate to be on time for my director's meeting. Everyone at the office would bring their lunch, and I took some of the food my mom made that Sunday. She had come home to babysit my children because the nanny was not good.

Her actions almost caused my daughter's death. Fortunately, my husband arrived home early and realized the house was filled with gas. He immediately took them out of the house. The Lord sent my husband home on time and saved precious lives.

Well, as I finished my lunch, I got a call from one of the spiritual seniors of our congregation.

She said, *"I wish you wouldn't put your food in the refrigerator. You should buy something when you are ready to eat."*

I began to reconsider what I had eaten, and she was correct - something about my food was different. In retrospect, there was something in it that was grainy but tasteless. The following morning, I again experienced recurring abdominal pain and vomiting, which was incessant. This episode was quite severe and led me to the hospital, where I was admitted with a diagnosis of an acute abdomen.

Evaluations revealed nothing, but the doctors decided that an operation was necessary. God, my Mighty Everlasting Father, was so gracious that He sent life-preserving warnings to me. Thank God for His clarity, and with a spirit of obedience, His warnings were heeded, so I'm still here today.

These warnings came in the following manner. First, a co-worker of my husband, who was also Christian, met him while he came to see me in the hospital. During a brief conversation, my husband relayed that his co-worker advised him to stand with his wife, supporting her in her decision to do whatever God says. I did not know the man in any way, nor did he know me or the reason for my hospitalization.

Secondly, my private office receptionist called my mom, informing her of her dream the night before. Her interpretation of that dream was for me not to have surgery because her dream revealed a specific demonic presence that would be harmful if I chose to have the surgery.

More importantly, while lying in the hospital bed, there were several meaningful experiences. The first came as a nursing assistant was attending to me. I did not need help, but as she wiped my back, she began to share encouraging stories about her husband, who had experienced injuries from a horrible car accident.

It was an accident from which God had miraculously delivered him. As she shared, she emphasized that God had healed him through the prayer of faith and constant reading of His word. I felt compelled to listen and did so with an expectant spirit.

God miraculously sent me these signs. I experienced another recommendation in which a powerful saint called and prayerfully encouraged me to trust in God as she shared her story of God's miraculous healing hand.

Then came the clincher, a call from a woman from my job. This one was too obvious to be unnoticed.

That is to say, if I had missed any previous warning, I could not miss this one. This incident spoke for itself. When I answered the call, she asked for my location, stating that she had some papers that needed my signature.

I was a bit reluctant and asked, *"Why now? I'm in the hospital."*

She paused for a moment stating that it was necessary.

So, I responded, *"OK, maybe God is preparing me for another position."*

She immediately replied, *"What position? You're going straight to heaven."*

I immediately felt a massive caution in my Spirit; thus, I asked, *"What do you mean by that?"*

After this question, there was complete silence. It seemed like an eternity, and I ultimately had to hang up.

But! Hallelujah to God; bright and early the following day, God sent His angel into my room. It was uncanny because there was a vase with flowers on the table, which just toppled spontaneously. Soon after, in walked a gentleman, and the strange thing about this was that person was dressed in *regular* clothing. The whole staff wears a uniform at the hospital. I had not called any service, but he came in with a mop. I was unsure how he got there and who informed him about the vase, but he came prepared to mop up that spill. As he was actively drying up, he began to talk with me. He started with two pointed *statements*.

The first was the following question, *"What are you reading?"*

I had two books on the nightstand. One was my Bible, and the other a book, 'Like a Mighty Wind, by Mel Tari. For me, the theme of this book was to trust in God and His word and very simply allow Him to do His work in and through our lives.

This book talked about a group of people who were fleeing from turbulent times in their village. As they were running, they came upon an uncrossable river. It was like a modern-day Jordan experience. However, God made a path by erecting a stone bridge from the river's depths, and they could go across to safety. I believed what I read because it was attributed to the power of Almighty God. And God is capable of resolving all seemingly impossible situations.

This gentleman said, *"These are good books. Keep reading but get up and see what God says to you in the morning."*

Folks! It is an understatement to say there was excitement in my Spirit. After his statement to me, I cannot recall how long I slept or even if I slept at all, but, in the morning, at around 5 AM, I remember looking over to my right when I saw an astonishing sight.

A hand was suspended in mid-air just above my side, holding a pouch like a money bag with pebbles reflected from inside. I looked at the hand, which remained still for a while. I then pressed my abdomen, which was surprisingly not painful even though I had been in much pain earlier that night.

I pressed my arm where the IV needle was inserted, and again there was no pain; it was as if the IV was not even there. I then realized that I had received supernatural healing. I began to pray in thankfulness. I could not wait for the doctors to come in for their rounds. When they came, I promptly refused the surgery offered and immediately told them I was going home because I was healed and felt better. One of them commented that the only healings he had seen were those done with his hands. I looked up at him briefly and said something that I believed came from God to him through my lips.

I said, *"It's only because you don't know the God I serve!"*

While in the hospital, I had two sets of visitors. One visit was from two brothers of faith who were members of the young adult group I chaired. While they were at the hospital with me, my prayer partner came, and we all embarked on a prayer session with Almighty God. During that session, the Lord revealed glad tidings for one of the young men, Tidings that were later actualized. Since then, God has continuously opened many doors for others.

After so many years of those miraculous experiences, I began to experience a new challenge. It was a little after 5 AM on a Tuesday; I did not have much sleep the night before. I found myself at another crossroads in life as others encouraged me to make a decision that was a bit problematic for me.

I remember praying about the transition from my neighborhood office practice. I had considered physical and spiritual assistance for my replacement. A young physician came in during that period but left approximately a year afterward. I might have inadvertently contributed to that since, deep in my heart; I was not ready to let go of the home-based neighborhood office I had started.

I have reached out to several others but am still trying to succeed. The handwriting was on the wall, but I hoped something would change. I had a desire in my heart, but it is not lining up for several reasons. First, my final hopes for a replacement were crushed when an NP who had agreed to consider my proposal began her stalling tactics. Her responses were initially forthcoming, but afterward, there was a long pause. I pressed on with a few promptings but still await progress. Finally, after I sent her a pre-COVID-19 e-mail, there came the *"BIG NO,"* a crushing response from her.

My husband kept telling me she did not want the office, but I did not see it that way. All I could see was that he wanted me to relocate in response to decisions we had made years before, but there were so many changes since I had made that agreement. My hope was crushed. I still feel terrible about leaving my clients, who seem so much physically, emotionally, and spiritually in need.

I, however, did not abandon them, for I directed them to other providers in the area. For me, God's answers are usually straightforward, but I cannot say I have heard from Him in a way that's understandable to me regarding this matter. Other family members have told me He has sent the answer, but I must listen attentively. The struggle of needing to know has had me alternating between pleading with God, staying awake at night, and being somewhat saddened. I trust that I have come down on the right side of things. Sometime after agonizing, inevitably or more precisely because of God-directed events, I wrote an office closure letter informing my patients of a specific closure date for my part-time office, which I had begun in 1983. Even after my assistant started mailing these out, there was still an element of uncertainty about this matter. However, following

God's word, I continued to pray fervently, trying to cast my burdens upon Him. I can only say that God has seen me through that valley, and I am now resting in Him.

My prayer is that you will also pray and rest in God when you come upon incomprehensible obstacles or difficult crossroads in life. You and I must strive to know the signs, voices, and warnings He provides. It is not always easy, but with His help, we will end up in the right place if we stay with God.

His word instructs us *'to trust in Him, the Lord, with all our heart and lean not unto our understanding.'* – (Proverbs 3: 6-7)

Sometimes, we fail to understand God's plans and signs, but let's continue to pray for strength and endeavor to trust Him at all times. Whether or not we can trace His path at the moment, remember that He is Sovereign and genuinely desires the best for us. We are directed to trust Him at all times. The office has been closed for a while now, and God's peace has overshadowed my doubts. I believe that closure has always been a part of God's plan. I just couldn't let go on my own. He became my strength in one of my weakest moments.

Chapter 4: Assignment and Revelations in the House of the Deep, Where God Directs He Always Provides

"But for those who are righteous, the way is not steep and rough. You are a God who does what is right, and you smooth out the path ahead of them."

(Isaiah. 26:7)

While writing, I am sitting and wondering. I cannot start without thanking my Great Almighty God for awakening me in my right mind with thoughts that are covered and kept by him. As I pondered, I was led to my assignment at a mid-Manhattan clinic. Interestingly, the poignant question was, *how did I get there?* This was the first I had heard of that facility, and I was unaware of its existence.

Nevertheless, the revelation came when I opened my house doors for our senior Pastor's arranged meetings. In that meeting was a representative from the Baptist convention. He was scheduled to prepare the Church body for renewal, but his presentation offered a personal clue to my path.

It's incredible how the Lord orders our steps. I recall sitting in our dining room at the Lay Renewal meeting arranged by the late Reverend Doctor Samuel G. Simpson. During that meeting, Ray Boggs, one of the directors in Lay Renewal, began his presentation with the story of Jesus' calling of His disciples in Luke Chapter 5:1-10. He mainly focused on Peter, but what resonated with me was Jesus' directive to Peter.

According to Luke's Gospel, the skilled fisherman Peter had toiled all night but had caught nothing. So, to his chagrin, this stranger is telling him to plunge out into the deep. For those of you who don't know the story well, let me summarize it for you. Peter was a very outspoken fisherman who was very good at his trade. However, he knew where to catch fish with a net which is usually not *"out in the deep."*

However, when he was approached and directed by Jesus to plunge out into the deep and let down his net for a catch, for a moment, Peter must have thought this was preposterous.

Still, somehow, at the directive of Jesus, he obeyed, saying, *"Master, we have toiled all night and have caught nothing: nevertheless, at thy word, I will let down the net."*

To his amazement, as well as that of his friends, as he obeyed, up came the net full and almost bursting with fish. At that moment, I felt alerted in my Spirit as if God told me to *"plunge out into the deep."*

I could only pause to wonder, *'Where is my deep?' 'Where should I plunge?'* I had no idea where to go with that train of thought.

A few days later, when I was getting ready for work, I was still thinking about that lingering question. It just wouldn't leave my mind. As I walked down the stairs from the porch of our Bronx home, I witnessed several spiritual alerts; the spiritual voice said that God was seeing me and that He had opened particular doors for me. But, in addition, only He alone can open those doors, and when He closes them, no one can open them.

Through the Apostle John, He says, "I know thy works: behold, I have set before thee an open door, and no man can shut it: for thou hast a little strength, and hast kept my word, and hast not denied my name."

(Revelation 3:8)

It is true when I tell you I did not have to look too hard or too long. Because later on, one of my Pediatric Residency preceptors, whom I did not previously know, advised me to participate in a facility for homeless runaway youth because there was availability for a clinical elective at that location. He was doing clinical work in a facility for homeless runaway youth, and I had to do some electives to complete my residency training year. I was keen to learn more about the needs of this population, so I signed up immediately. I was then prompted with an alert that connected my previous thoughts of the deep. I then understood where to go, for this place was my *"deep."*

However, I was surprised that this would be my assignment for over three decades. There in that facility, I had a wealth of exposure and experiences. It truly opened the door to my training ground for ministry. But, after completing that elective, I applied for a fellowship – advanced training in allergy and immunology at Einstein Hospital, which was for minority students. I was one of the final two candidates during the last interview. The other candidate was Jewish and, in my opinion, should not have been classified as a minority. But, on the other hand, in our society, I was seen as a minority.

Well, I was surprised when he was favored by the third interviewer and was awarded the fellowship. However, I was very disappointed because I thought such a clerkship would facilitate my desire to find a cure for cancer. This disease had stolen my dear Granny's life. This fellowship guided me in this direction.

Over the years, I considered it more my desire, for my heavenly Father had other plans. His plan was not the cure for physical cancer; it involved something that would be far more significant and comprehensive.

His plans included that I work to find and administer the remedy for spiritual cancer. A debilitating illness that damages the mind, body, and spirit of a person. What better place for this to happen than a facility where many of our battered, bruised, and lost young people, primarily young women, were located? A place where many would be available at any given time, with minds that were inflicted with many upsetting wounds; Some were sexually abused, others were addicted to drugs, and many did not complete school due to early pregnancies and were often thrown out of their homes by their parents.

I remember a young lady, and I believe God sent her to me because of how she came. So, I had a flipchart on my desk with Bible verses, and each day I would flip it over to read and digest at least one verse before beginning my day; it was my habit. I did not know that children at the facility were also looking at it. So, one day this young lady came up to me and asked if I could explain one of the passages of the Bible to her.

I did, and since then, she would come into my office to talk to me and ask questions almost daily. She was initially furious and upset; I had seen her behavior and heard her spitting in the face of one of the male doctors. However, nobody understood why she behaved like that.

I later learned that she did not want any man near her for any reason at all. She was traumatized by the sexual abuse perpetrated by her stepfather. As a result, she became pregnant and delivered that baby. It was heartbreaking to see her suffer through bouts of anger, so along with counseling, I asked her to come to the Church, and she did come.

After attending for a while, she accepted the Lord and got baptized. I had become the source for her to understand God's plan as I guided her through a study of His word. She listened to me and later developed a relationship that resulted in marriage. Her first child, one that she was tempted to abort, became a source of strength for her. That child grew in grace, went into the army, and bought a house for her mother. Despite the negativity in that pregnancy, her child's birth became one of her greatest blessings. It was a part of the spiritual cure.

After completing my residency training, I worked at the Pediatric Emergency Department at Metropolitan Hospital for a brief period. Then, I worked part-time at the Health Services Department of a specialized Clinic in Manhattan under the leadership of a kind-hearted Medical Director. After a few years of working there, one night, I had quite a lucid dream. In that dream, I was invited for lunch by my director. I hesitated at first but then accepted the invitation.

As we were walking together down a flight of stairs, he confided that he had to leave the agency because he had contracted AIDS. Then, he handed me a bouquet of beautiful flowers and said he was turning over the clinic to me because I would be an excellent asset to the place. However, as I woke up, I shared the dream with my mom, prayer partner, and confidante. After that, I never really thought about it until approximately one year later, when my dream became a reality.

My dream was carried out precisely the way it was revealed to me. That is to say, my director had to leave, and I was put in charge of the clinic because I was an asset. All of this was revealed in my dream already and with such specificity, except that my kind-hearted leader was not suffering from natural AIDS but a spiritual condition not unlike its natural counterpart.

I was not only surprised but extremely awed that God had revealed it to me with such specificity. So, I continued to seek God's face regarding the situation, our Covenant keeping God, the God who says: *"Before they call, I will answer; while they are still speaking, I will hear."* (Isaiah 65:24)

As I assumed my new position, not everyone in the office was happy seeing me at my director's place. Among many, one specific lady gave me such a gut-wrenching response. At the particular time of our encounter, I could not process clearly what was happening because I was dismayed. It happened while I was alone in the clinic's pharmacy with her. She was a nurse practitioner trainee who was undoubtedly not as educationally prepared or skilled as me, a pediatrician. That is to say: I was her senior in many ways.

However, as I recall, I now understand that the lady was quite obnoxious as she challenged her director's competency. I was her director, and she said I did not deserve such a position because the previous director was better suited. I would never comprehend why she said it because everyone knew the previous director was not trained in Pediatrics or Adolescent medicine while I was.

I quietly turned toward the door when she finished talking, or should I say after she accosted me. My eyes welled up with tears because what she said was quite hurtful. Before I could reach for the door handle, I was promptly spun around by none other than the Holy Spirit, the Third Person of the Godhead, because out of my mouth came the following words:

"I need to say something to you! You can say what you want! You may not understand it, but God Almighty revealed this assignment to me in a dream approximately twelve months before our director approached me. You don't know Him and, therefore, wouldn't understand how He speaks to His children. So if you do nothing else, you better get to know Him. He is real, and He sent his son to die for our sins so that we may have a life with Him in Heaven. You and I are nothing without Him, and we will be confined to hell if we refuse to accept the path He has laid out for

deliverance. I might have said more, but I can't quite recall."

I left immediately after saying the words God had put in my mind. A later reflection on this incident revealed that I could have terminated her. I was the senior preceptor, but she felt she had the right to accost and demean me because she had been brainwashed to view people of color a certain way. She believed I was less than her only because of my complexion. She said I did not deserve the position because I was Black and the previous director was better just because he was White. This was not the first time I have directly experienced prejudice and discrimination, no matter how accomplished or authoritative I have been.

After numerous years, I've realized that behavior similar to that of the above woman is not foreign. Most people, like me, experience it as a norm in our society. Furthermore, I have realized that it's not only because we look different but because many of us are very good at what we do and are seen as a threat. But we are good at what we do simply because we have applied ourselves to our God-created design.

In addition, many think of us as emotionless creatures incapable of being hurt. For example, I remember a clinician saying male babies don't feel pain like the more mature males do. As a result, infant boys can be circumcised without pain blockers. These are heinous patterns that I have observed and experienced, personally in thought and deed, throughout my educational journey and during postgraduate training. In reflecting, I believe it happened because I was too trusting or naïve to understand people's intentions for what they are and continue to be even today.

Over the years, I have realized that it is a false notion that others have attempted to normalize. The fabricated deficiencies and lies about people of darker complexions must be eradicated. Satan, the Father of lies and our archenemy, has blinded the eyes of the self-acclaimed privileged, and so they reject and neglect the wisdom of God in his creation of beauty in variety,

"How many are your works, Lord, in wisdom, you made them all; the earth is full of your creatures.... living things both large and small."

-   (Psalm 104:24-25)

Unfortunately, due to a lack of appreciation, there are disunity, friction, schisms, and wars, as some people consider others to be subhuman. It is a tragedy since the gifts deposited in each person are for the betterment of the whole human race. I have had many experiences in this regard. I have won many battles and defended many individuals for them to be considered and validated for their value.

Although painful, these battles must be seen as spiritual experiences or warfare from which others may learn and grow.

In addition, my numerous experiences and their many lessons will require volumes for them to be documented. Although many of these experiences were very painful, several were interspersed with joyful and productive moments because there are good caring people in every race. No matter how much negligence or hatred per se I experienced, I will never regret my assignment at that facility because it was beneficial not only to homeless youth and children but to my family as well.

I have had hectic routines; right from the start of my career, I wanted to be free, so I could worship on Sunday in the Church and spend more time with my family. In addition, I needed to have more time that I could invest in my children. The good Lord granted my prayers as He has always done. So, instead of working long hours in the hospital, I chose a four-day workweek for my God-directed assignment at the Manhattan Clinic. Hence, I could spend more time with my family and Church.

Since I came to know the Lord as Savior, I have been actively engaged in Church and was a choir member, singing in the contralto section. My daughter's friend told her I held on to my children too tightly and needed to cut some slack for them. But later on, it was evident that my stance was appropriate when I saw what happened to others. I was not unnecessarily strict because I had to teach them many vital guidelines, just like I taught the young lady and others at the clinic.

It was the Doctor Cosby era when it was popular to have doctors available in the neighborhood. So, for the benefit of my neighbors, I established an office on the lower level of our triplex house. I worked three to four evenings and half days on Saturdays from 1983 until 2013 while simultaneously working daytime in the clinic in lower Manhattan.

I remember once having a group of young people who tested HIV positive. It was during the 80s that HIV was rampant, and little was known about it. However, God taught me and propelled me to learn and read more about this matter. I taught myself sufficiently about STDs because I was not told anything regarding them during the hospital training. Another resident asked me why I was reading so much about STDs.

He didn't know then, nor did I, but God was equipping me for the upcoming situation at the Manhattan clinic. Hence, when the time came, I was well prepared. In addition, He sent me a medical assistant from a Pentecostal Church who believed in the power, presence, and personhood of the Holy

Spirit at a time when I did not know much about His personhood.

The Holy Spirit helped me through prayers and many revelations to treat these children. Later, after being accidentally stuck by a used, un-discarded needle, I got myself tested and was very nervous about the result. However, thanks to God, I tested negative and could remain on the job.

There was another incident with a very young woman addicted to drugs. I remember praying for her and her kids, who were already placed into the foster care system, where they would be taught and cared for while the lady went to a facility for young women. This woman's life was transformed magically. I used to send care packages to her every month to encourage her.

When she returned to visit her kids, who were in foster care, I could barely recognize her transformation. Then sadly, several days, maybe weeks after she saw me at the clinic, I got the news that she had been strangled to death in a park while hanging out with past acquaintances. It was horrific news, but what gave me peace was that although she was absent from her body, her spirit was saved. I believe this because I remembered praying a specific verse for her while she was away at the facility for young women. I did not know then why I was directed to speak 1 Corinthians 5:5 over her life. However, in reflection, the Apostle Paul stated, *"The Corinthian Church should turn over a man caught in gross sexual immorality to Satan for the destruction of the flesh so that his spirit may be saved on the day of the Lord. This indicated to me that the young woman was most likely removed from the earthly realm at a time when she could be saved.*

I was told that the young woman had nobody but her grandmother, who couldn't afford her funeral expenses. Hence, the government had to pay for her burial. It was a painful moment, but God has done his best for her.

This is why I want to tell these stories to my children and all young people so they can see how God has guided me. As they read, they too can note how God directed me to study and prepare myself with the information I did not know so that when I plunged into the deep, I would have the data when needed. By reading my stories, they, too, can be strengthened to trust God's guidance. The director in charge was not trained in Pediatrics or Adolescent medicine, so he appreciated my presence.

I remember he handed me a case that was presented to him, and he left the patient in my hands because he trusted my capabilities. I also remember God sent an assistant to tell me more about the Holy Spirit. I know He is real because of all these incidents and revelations. They have all helped me to trust more fervently in the Holy Spirit's presence and power. Then, again, I was reminded of another woman I advised to reconsider her decision to abort the child in her womb.

I told her God had blessed her with the child for a purpose. I told her I did not know the reason, but I knew He would strengthen her and guide her on the right path.

She replied, *"You all live in your big houses, and when you go home at night, you don't think about us."*

Those words stayed with me; I carried their weight home with me.

My husband wondered why I worried about those children and would often ask, *"Do you want them to come and live with you?"*

I would respond, *"According to the dictates of the agency, I can't, but God can and will provide them with a home where they will be safe if we pray and act."*

I remember praying from the depths of my heart in the far corners of the Church, and I would not think or care who heard me; I frequently cried out for a home for one particular young woman. As a result, her child grew up and subsequently got to a place where she could buy her own home. So I know God answers prayers.

My journey has taught me that no matter our decisions and how good we are to people, some will always criticize our personal choices. Unfortunately, I have been a victim of this criticism all my life; working out of my house was attacked by those who knew nothing about God's calling on my life, my detailed conversations with Him, or my need to be available for my children.

That is the thing about people; they will know nothing about your life and will not believe anything except their outlook and assumptions. They think they have answers, but the true and living God Himself declares that His gifts are uniquely distributed to His children for the assignments He has chosen for each of us.

Ephesians 4:7 clearly states: *"But to each of us, grace has been given as Christ apportioned it."*

Similarly, **Ephesians 2:10 states,** *"We are His workmanship created in Christ Jesus for good works, which God prepared beforehand so that we would walk in them."*

So, my children, please note that although those criticisms were painful, God's grace and strength have brought me through and will continue to do so for you, too, if you trust in Him and have faith in His plans with all your heart. There have been many revelations, teachable, and protective moments I have had with both my biological children and my God-given spiritual children.

The Almighty God has directed all these; if I were not available in those crucial moments, I do not know what would have happened to them.

They would have been in serious trouble unless God had sent help from another source, but He indeed provided all that was needed.

"Where God guides, He provides."

– Isaiah 58:11

Chapter 5: My Initial Introduction to the House of the Deep

This is our **B** moment. Our moment to **be** still...to **be** fed by the Word of God...to **be** grateful.

Trust in and rely confidently on the Lord with all your heart, and do not rely on your insight or understanding.

(Proverbs 3:5 AMP)

Introducing this particular 'house in the deep' may seem like a chance event, but nothing happens by chance.

Many people will say that coincidence and happenstance shape and navigate a person. However, in reality, God establishes those events that we think are coincidences. If we trust God's word, we'll grow in understanding that. He clearly states that He has plans for us, plans to prosper us and not harm us, plans to give us hope and a future (Jeremiah 29:11). He has also numbered our days, and He will fulfill every purpose He has for us. God starts numbering our days and assigns us our purpose in life even before our birth.

Christ, my Savior, has guided my steps throughout my life. He has been ordering the directions and path He has chosen for me. As I started noticing all the signs, I grew more in understanding Him and His plans for me. Am I always perfect at doing that? No, of course not. But I trust Him because He says clearly that He has plans for us, and I only need to keep my eyes on His signs and directives.

"He has plans for us, plans to prosper and not harm us, to give us hope and a future."

(Jeremiah 29:11)

My first exposure came from one of my preceptors at Metropolitan Hospital. Due to a train strike, He had to drive from the Bronx to Manhattan for work and offered some students a ride. I accepted the offer, and my husband dropped me off at his place. So I got in his car, and we drove to work together. It was amazing how I met him. I was in my last year of residency training when this professor told the class about a rotation available through his work in the city's heart.

He continued his presentation and discussed the assignment for any willing person. As explained previously, the introduction piqued my interest. Still, that interest was first ignited at a lay renewal in-house meeting where I was directed to *"plunge out into the deep."*

That deep was a haven for those in crisis – a multifunctional homeless facility. My experience in that place was overwhelming; I had the opportunity to pray as I had never prayed before, to deliver and receive lessons from uncanny persons and the most unusual circumstances. There was a Chapel, and the Catholic Priest in charge had no reservations about my request to pray at the Chapel during lunch breaks.

While there, The Lord, our Magnificent God, sent two other folks to join me in prayers. One became my medical assistant, and the other worked on the residential floor. After a while, the second one stopped coming to the Chapel, and soon after, I heard that he had left the job. Nevertheless, my medical assistant and I continued because God preserved our position at the clinic. Many people were laid off during that period, but our jobs remained open. I believe it was God's will for us to stay in the deep. He preserved our jobs at the clinic so that we could do His bidding. He protected us and gave us strength for the journey.

One such lesson came to mind as I realized my position at that facility was not a job but a God-directed assignment in line with His calling on my life, and He certainly does not make any mistakes. Therefore, every connection was to line me up for that placement, which became my long-term job after a while. While there, I had many lifesaving revelations. Some occurred while I was praying, and others came through practical experiences.

Many of these experiences strengthened me so that I would not quit my assignment prematurely, and others were meant to help our misplaced and wounded children. I stayed at this clinic because God directed me; even though I could have made more money elsewhere, He managed my income.

During my time at the clinic, I had many experiences with young, needy people. One of these had to do with a young man who had severe seizures, otherwise known as epilepsy. He would fall anywhere and anytime, whether in the elevator, residential floors, or courtyard. As the assigned physician, I would be called to his aid. In addition, I was often called to administer treatment.

I later got to know that this young man was a graduate of a Bible school in Manhattan. One day, he fell and was twitching a lot. I was not afraid but realized his condition was very critical. I stayed with him, prayed for him, and cared for him. We gave him the necessary injections and adjusted his medications. Finally, it seemed that he had become better, so he left the agency, and I had never heard from him for years.

After a while, I was invited to speak at my medical assistant's graduation ceremony at a Bible College in Manhattan. I was standing in the hallway with other people when I saw a young man approaching me with a big smile.

I asked him, *"Do I know you?"*

He replied, *"Don't you remember me?"*

I was amazed because I could not recall who he was. Then, after a pause, he finally told me his name, but even that did not ring a bell.

Then, he smiled, *"I'm the one who fell out in the elevator, and you took care of me several times."*

This was when I realized that this was the man from many years back because his gums were enlarged from the side effects of medicines. Well, it was such a blessing to see him grow and graduate.

Another experience involved a young man who entered my office with intense pruritus.

He came in screaming at the top of his lungs, *"They're biting me. Get them off of me, get them off me!"*

He was thrashing and flailing around. I was afraid as my medical assistant was not in the room. In attending to him, I took a brief history. I examined him, only to note there were no bugs, and he was hallucinating. At that moment, this young man had experienced a seemingly accurate perception of something not present. It was a result of the drugs he had been taking, which had him thinking that the bugs were always biting him all over his body. I was in my earlier years and desperately wanted to help as much as possible, so I began to share how God could help him in his situation.

If only he would trust and believe in God.

He responded by throwing up his arms, moving erratically, and shouting, *"I want to hear nothing about God. Get them off of me!"*

His actions were frightening, and they certainly evoked fear in me. I was a bit distressed but gave him the necessary stabilizers and called in an emergency notice. The paramedics came and transported him via ambulance to the hospital. As I sat at my desk, I privately made a fear-evoked decision that I would never tell anyone else, at that place, about God.

Family and friends, I tell you that it is what Satan, our enemy, wants us to do. Satan does not want us to share God's word with others who need it the most. Yes, this is precisely what demons want us to do; they want us to quit and not guide people on how they can get out of the pit and escape the everlasting place of punishment that awaits the ones who reject Christ. As we have noted in our society, people have perished and are perishing due to a lack of knowledge (Proverbs 28:18).

Without the word of God and its proper application, people go their own way, and I say once again that ignoring God's way is to ignore the way of life and blessings. We all need wisdom, knowledge, and understanding.

The Bible says, *"We all need wisdom, the master key to success and abundant life."* (Proverbs 4:7).

I needed help in the form of wisdom that day, and true to His nature and word, our miraculous God sent support which was greatly needed. I will admit it was only in retrospect that I saw this. But, immediately after the terrifying first young man was taken to the hospital by ambulance, a calm, sedate young White man walked in. I needed help that day, and true to His word, our miraculous God was right on time. I sat at my desk in awe when I realized God had not given up on me. Yet it was only in retrospect that I saw this. Indeed, God helps us in our weakest moments. He knows when assistance is greatly needed.

The word of God declares,

"My people are destroyed for lack of knowledge. Therefore, because you have rejected knowledge, I have rejected you from being a Priest to me. And since you have forgotten the law of your God, I will also forget your children."

(Hosea 4: 6)

A review of the young man's chart revealed no reason for this young man to be in a homeless shelter.

So, as I usually do for every patient, I looked at him and asked, *"Why are you here?"*

His response shocked me, *"I'm here to see how my sister is doing."*

At that moment, I raised my eyebrows and asked, *"Your sister, does your sister work at the facility?"*

There was, however, no need for a verbal answer because as I looked at him, I realized something unusual was happening. After all, it appeared as if I was looking straight into the deepest, most transparent, most peaceful blue eyes I had ever seen.

However, he again responded while looking at me, *"I am here to see how my sister is doing."*

I was amazed by looking at him.

His history and examination were exceptionably clean, so he was discharged. This young man left the room, and I observed something remarkable as I watched him move down the hall. This young man was not walking. He was levitating. It was a sight I will never forget. Soon afterward, the Holy Spirit showed me He had sent an angel to strengthen me. Here was a true example of His promise to provide help in times of need (Psalm 46:1-3) and His affirmation that He will never leave or forsake me/us. (Deuteronomy 4:31)

When we are in any destitute situation, He will send help to get us back on the designated path. And when we do not understand, He will guide us with His righteous right hand. I believe this experience was heaven-sent help from God.

I knew then and there that I did not have to worry, no matter the difficulties. I was assured that He was always going to be with me. So many more incidents taught me that He had put me in that clinic to help His people. It was the home in the deep for me. He kept affirming His presence in my life as I continued serving His young people.

Through this incident, He left a new awakening of His spirit in me; and one of His angels ministered to me; since then, I have never felt afraid to minister to young people when I remember that I have been given the knowledge and strength to walk in obedience to God's will and purpose.

"So do not fear, for I am with you; do not be dismayed, for I am your God. I will strengthen you and help you; I will uphold you with my righteous right hand."

– (Isaiah 41:10–12 NIV)

My introduction to this place in the heart of the city was ordered. Every step and every encounter was calculated and provided by God. All of this happened to strengthen and give me the necessary wisdom to address the needed care. I later spent more time counseling people mentally as well. He guided and highlighted how it would be done because He assigned me to heal people physically, mentally, and spiritually.

Healing only one of these areas was not enough for truly broken individuals; all three areas had to be addressed. This I tried to accomplish through my prayers and actions. Many of the young people started coming to the Chapel. We prayed for them as they came. This was my introduction, given by the Merciful, to the house of deep.

Family and friends, God's presence and activities in my life are for our edification, our instruction, morally and intellectually.

Let us all allow Him to bless, protect and strengthen us.

This you can do simply by asking at any time of the day. Undoubtedly, He resides within us and listens to every word we say.

Chapter 6: Angelic Visitations

"For he will command his angels concerning you to guard you in all your ways. They will bear you up on their hands lest you strike your foot against a stone."

– (Psalm 91: 11-12)

Most of the time, God sends an angel in human form to us in extreme times of pain, loss, or grief. They are sent to offer us hope, to guide and protect us. I believe angelic interventions are life-transforming events as God promises to assist us when we honor Him and live morally. After all, God is always working on our behalf; whether we realize it or not, there is a spiritual realm constantly around us.

I remember being rescued and guided by angelic visitations when I was completely unaware of the situation. On one such occasion, early in the morning, I was on my way to work. While driving down 233rd Street, the main street in our area, the traffic was heavy, and there was much congestion. Then, from a distance, I heard the tooting of a horn. As I looked briefly in the direction of the sound, there to my left sat my Pastor, The Rev Dr. Samuel Simpson, in his car next to mine.

It was a cold morning; the light had caught all of us. It was when Rev. Simpson asked me through my closed window, *"What is the matter?"*

From that encounter, I realized that he was trying to get my attention, but for some reason, he could not do so until we came to the stop light. It puzzled me a little because, in the back of my mind, I wondered if I was driving in a daze.

On another occasion, I was driving across 234th Street. I went across the sign at the intersection, where I looked both ways and saw no approaching vehicles. However, all of a sudden, a vehicle was approaching my car. I had no idea where the vehicle came from because I had already looked to my left and then right; then, as was my habit, I turned to glance to my left once more, only to see that a car was barreling toward me beyond the highest possible speed for a local road.

Based on its speed, it was as if the car was driving on a highway. Therefore, any observer would surmise that there would be an impact.

At the intersection of the two streets, a young man on the sidewalk asserted this as he shouted, *"Blow wow!"*

The Jamaican community uses this well-known phrase when something horrible is going to happen. I surely thought there would be an awful crash, but the fact that it didn't happen was nothing less than a miracle, so I must say that it had to be God's divine intervention. He protected me from a possible horrendous crash as I was in line for a dangerous collision. But to my astonishment, the car approaching me veered off at a 90-degree angle.

The man behind the wheel miraculously made a sharp left turn that moved the car away from me toward the sidewalk, where it almost hit the young man who shouted, *"Blow, wow!"*

From the corner of my eye, I saw when he scampered out of the way of the oncoming car. As a result, we were all spared from a potentially catastrophic accident. I can only believe that an angel had intervened.

All I could think about was the verse in which King David in Psalm 34: 7 says, *"The angel of the Lord encamps around those that fear Him and delivers them."*

During those difficult times, I realized that angelic encounters protected me. Another day when I was driving toward the highway in the same direction, I came to the intersection one block away from the previous incident between 234th Street and White Plains Road. As customary, I looked left, right, and again quickly to my left.

Since no vehicles were in sight, I moved slowly from the intersecting point toward the middle of the road. Then, surprisingly a car approached and almost touched mine on the passenger side. The car's front end was just a few inches from my door.

Inside the vehicle, a gentleman raised his hands in surprise to ask, *"What's happening here?"*

To this day, I still need to learn where and how the car appeared there. In retrospect, the vehicle may have been parked and pulled out after moving from behind the stop sign. Nevertheless, to my relief, God had once again spared me from an accident.

On another occasion, I was driving across 233rd Street toward the highway. After completing one-third of the large block occupied by Woodlawn Cemetery, I saw a car speeding toward me from the opposite direction. When the Spirit of God alerted me that the vehicle was not about to stop, I obeyed and floored the gas pedal. It all happened just in time.

The Holy Spirit had intervened by quickening my spiritual ears and my spirit of obedience to move my car swiftly. In my rearview mirror, I saw the other vehicle moving across the same area of the road I was on just seconds before. Someone else would be writing a different story about me if I had not responded to God's prompting to move forward quickly.

I realized that during that period of my life. A destructive pattern was emerging against my entire family and me.

However, I kept my mind on the directives mentioned in Psalm 100:3, which states, ***"Know that*** *the Lord is God; He made us, and we are His people and the sheep of His pasture."*

And so *"When the enemy comes in like a flood, I was assured that the Spirit of the LORD will lift a standard against him."* Isaiah 59:19

The above verses tell me that we are His possession, and God is always ready to set up His banner of protection over us.

Another early morning, I was driving from the service road onto the entrance of the West Side Highway, and again, as I got right in the merging of the lane to get on the highway, my car stalled. Several cars were whizzing by me, and I was terror-stricken. The engine refused to budge even after I tried to restart the vehicle.

I could do nothing, so I kept pleading silently to God. Finally, I turned the key over again, hoping the Holy Spirit would intervene, but nothing happened. However, soon after my plea, a car slowed and came beside me.

I could hear the gentleman say, *"Sister having car trouble! Help is on the way."*

I moved my gaze at him, expecting that he would get out of the car and offer to help, but to my surprise, he drove on. While wondering who would help me, I remembered noticing that the gentleman speaking was White and had no disinclination about calling me his sister. Therefore, in trust, I again raised my inner voice to God and pleaded for assistance.

As a result, in faith, I followed my heart and turned the key again. The car hesitated, and the engine cranked up and continued to hum. I was fascinated, but my inner voice cautioned me not to continue on the highway but to get off at the next exit just a few feet away.

When I exited the ramp and made a right turn, the car again slowed, and the engine sputtered. Eventually, it stopped again behind a parked vehicle with the hood up as if it was in trouble, but it was not. Instead, the car was waiting with a God-sent attendant to address my troubled situation.

I tried to restart the car, but it just would not happen.

Finally, an African American gentleman approached my window, and his words were the same, *"Sister having car trouble. Help is on the way."*

I was so flustered at that moment that I was in no condition to hear what he had to say, as the car had been troubling me since the morning. So I began to rattle off that I had been having a terrible morning.

He said, *"Don't worry."*

My response was, *"You don't understand. I'm going to 41st Street and 10th Avenue – traffic is bad, and I will be late."*

He repeated, *"Don't worry."*

He came around, lifted the hood of my car, and to my amazement, he did something that changed the course of my day. It was just like a miracle had happened. The engine responded, and the car was ready to roll. But, as I hesitated, he again assured me the car would take me to 41st Street and 10th Avenue and even back home.

Again, I was amazed, yet with some concern, I said, *"Okay, thank you."*

For a moment, I wasn't sure what exactly had happened. Still, I knew it was something supernatural because when I looked back in my rearview mirror, hoping to catch a glimpse of the person, I couldn't see any stalled car on the side, nor was a man standing there.

As I looked back at the situation, I came to believe that other angels had again assisted me.

To the readers of the books, I would like to inform you that the Spirit of God is always accurate, and His angels are assigned to help us. God offers His pure love through His angels and commands those faithful spirits to guard us in all our ways. However, as He said, the car took me to both locations without halting.

There are ministering spirits all around us.

Another proof was that my prayer partner and I went out to get lunch on a warm day. During our walk, we discussed how important it was to treat others with kindness because we unknowingly could be entertaining the angels. Just then, we came across a Chinese restaurant. As we entered, a man came into the restaurant and asked if someone would help him buy a meal. I looked at him and inquired what he preferred to eat. He shared his desire, and I told him to get what he wanted as I would pay for it.

After he got his food, he said, *"Yes, after you don't know whom you're buying this lunch for, you may be entertaining angel unawares."*

I was shocked because he used an expletive that didn't fit a Godly person, even though he had correctly expressed the directives about hospitality to angels, as seen in Hebrews 13:2. The incident spoke volumes. I realized then that God constantly reminds us to treat everyone kindly and help those in need when possible.

My husband experienced something similar, which I can only describe as an angelic visitation with grace and favor. My husband has a keen sense of God-directed awareness. He shared that something made him uneasy while returning to work from his lunch break. He went on to say that before he approached a specific intersection, a profound sense of apprehension came upon him after he had narrowly avoided hitting a cat that had run in front of his car. He wasn't superstitious, so he only considered it after the incident.

Furthermore, he noticed nothing in sight as he looked around cautiously. Then suddenly, he noticed a car speeding peculiarly toward him. Upon seeing this, he mustered great efforts to escape the vehicle, but he was not fast enough, and the car hit the back panel of his van. It seemed as if the other man was injured, so the ambulance took him to the hospital. My husband reported this incident to his bus company following standard procedures.

However, after waiting for a response from his company, nothing happened. It was as if the incident never occurred and got erased from the record. It was evident that heavenly intervention buffered the impact on his car and that God intervened again to save his life and clear his history.

Moreover, as stated in **Romans 8:31**: *"If God is for us, who can be against us?"*

The next event is very dear to my heart because it has to do with my children and the children of the Bronx Baptist Ministry. My children were on their way home from a borough-wide presentation when they experienced a delay. My husband and I received no calls from the people in charge, so we tried our best to sleep.

It wasn't easy, but we must have fallen asleep, and I experienced a vision early in the morning. The picture I saw was genuinely alarming for me. I viewed a hard-blowing breeze; the tall van was stalled on the bridge with the children. I could see it swaying back and forth in a boisterous howling wind.

I woke up immediately and cried to God, praying:

"God Almighty, Everlasting God, please send help from your sanctuary for my children. Our children are in that van, and they are in danger. Father, please send help! Thank you in Jesus' Mighty name."

It was almost morning when I received the call that the Southern Baptist missionary had relayed that the van had run out of gas. A consideration of the event revealed that my arousal to pray was God's call for me to participate in the work he was about to commence on their behalf. I was convinced of this since the timing of help coincided with the timing of our prayers.

Betty Joe shared that as she stood by the van with the hood open. Help arrived in the form of a gentleman who assisted them by flipping a switch from the empty to the full gas tank. She further mentioned that she was unaware of the two gas tank-equipped vans, but God sent His angel, and the children could complete their journey safely. It is again a reminder that God aids children in sickness and needs. There have been several such occasions in which God intervened on my behalf.

I hesitated to speak about another realization that became apparent when I was about seven. However, because God has been so generous to my family and to me specifically, I believe that sharing it can help people understand God's strength, grace, mercy, and forgiveness for others.

Nevertheless, I now realize that the Lord had a particular assignment I needed to know about. I also now know that He had put His hand on my life. This realization came in several ways; first, my sister took great interest in my abilities. She commenced nursing, and I was fascinated with her books because I love reading. As my sister noticed this, she fanned those flames and guided me, which allowed me to develop my skills.

Subsequently, I remember the women holding ministry meetings in my home rotationally. I can recall that most of the time, I was the only child in those meetings, listening to the wisdom and prayers. As a result, I grew in numerous ways at the girl's club of my Church, leading to my transformation. I was drawn to the sciences and math during my teenage years, but little did I know that my interest was being molded in a specific direction. Meanwhile, one of my sisters had relocated to England to continue her studies, and I strived for excellence and achieved honors in high school.

I was preparing for the next leg of my journey: a plane ride that brought me to my sister's apartment in the U.S.A.. Upon my arrival in the U.S. in 1969, my first step was finding a spiritual home. At that time, I started attending the Honeywell Baptist Church. Before leaving my Church in Jones Town, Kingston, Jamaica, I was directed to that Church by the elders there because the Honeywell Baptist Church's Pastor was originally a Jones Town Baptist Church member. Despite several obstacles and trials, I stayed there and worshipped because, during that journey, the Lord revealed that He had me there for a specific purpose.

This became clearer, for on a particular Sunday, while I was ministering, I heard the words of the Holy Spirit within me.

It said, *"I have you here to show people the power of the Holy Spirit."*

In determining my next steps, I shared my thoughts with Pastor Simpson. He directed me to a lawyer, who guided me and gave me a few options for my journey.

After I talked to my lawyer, I decided to seek permanent residency instead of a student visa. I was allowed to work with a family with two little boys whose caretaker was injured. They agreed to be a patron for residency status on my behalf as long as I was watchful over their two sons until their caretaker recovered from her surgery. I was grateful for this opportunity, and their names remain unforgettable.

Due to a chain of events, I realized that the former caretaker would soon want to return to her job. And just as I thought, I was released after a few months. I immediately took the opportunity to commence the journey on my education path. I applied to Hunter College and worked part-time at May's Department Store, where I met a young man who later became my husband.

Looking back, I can confirm the words of encouragement from **Romans 8:28, which says, *"All things work together for good to those who love the Lord and are called according to his purpose."***

In the early years of living with my sister, I noticed that life did not always produce for many of us the things we seemed to deserve. Sometimes, we even go against God's leading and other well-meaning voices to our detriment. As a result, we make choices that sometimes cause us more harm than good.

Once, while I was with my sister, a woman stared at me strangely. Then, looking me up and down, she made a statement without knowing or caring about its long-lasting impact.

She said, *"This child will give you much trouble."*

I was deeply affected by these words and felt incredibly wounded and angry. I vowed then and there to myself, my family, and God that I would not fail and, more importantly, I would not live up to what she had thought of me.

My warning is: *don't let negative words define you or your path.*

As stated in **Ephesians 5:6,** ***"Let no one deceive you with empty words, for because of such things, God's wrath comes on those who are disobedient."***

Chapter 7: Cultural Biases and the Blatant Expressions of Pain

"But even if you should suffer for righteousness, you are blessed: And do not fear their intimidation, and do not be troubled."

– 1 Peter 3:14

Pain and suffering come in waves; they are inevitable and often give a little time in between before the next one arrives.

We all must know and accept that pain is sometimes allowed by God, although He is not the cause of pain and suffering. He will enable it when we do wrong or when He wants to teach valuable lessons. It is crucial to accept that pain is inevitable in life, no matter how we deal with it. Most people do not know how to deal with suffering or how to prepare themselves for the next one waiting in line. They fail to realize that tough times bring learning opportunities.

People fail to acknowledge that their development may be stunted because they have disconnected themselves from the true giver of life. People need to recognize that their growth and deliverance may be restricted because they have detached themselves from the guidelines established by the true life-giver. A person's emotional and spiritual growth is directly linked with divine progress because everything works together for good and teaches us life's meaning and purpose.

As we all know, pain comes in all sorts, and it may not be easy to comprehend at the specific time it appears. Many of us have suffered through the shackles of pain and torment because of people at several stages of life. The psychological toll on a person discriminated against or looked down upon is often more than one can imagine. Discrimination often treads way because of the differences in a person's ethnicity, color, class, and creed, and many are losing their way because of these pressures, but with God, we can surmount those tough times.

I have already mentioned the pain I went through during medical school, which I received from students and teachers. I have witnessed the assault and robbery of my hard work, sacrificial time, and God-given talent during my residency training. A White supervisor tricked me into giving my work to another White-skinned resident as she pretended to care. I willingly gave my work out of the unquestioning nature of my heart. However, I was betrayed as she presented my work as her own while I sat there, listening to every word of my work from someone else's mouth.

This incident shattered me as I was mystified to see how a person could reach such a high level of evil.

Especially knowing that she had absolutely nothing to do with the material being presented yet was able to stand there boldly receiving all my accolades for recorded details which cost me much time, with no credit given to me.

Another incident where I was challenged face-to-face due to cultural biases was when a Russian woman interacted with me. I went to take one of my rare classes in which she was present; she was a good dancer working with the owner of a dance studio. My husband had set up the classes with that studio because he felt lonely while I was in New York. Even though she was a dancer there, she seemed more like a babysitter for the owner's young daughter.

After a particular class ended, she came directly at me to say, *"I hear that you are from a country where people live in huts with dirt floors and thatched roofs."*

I was shaken to the core. I raised an eyebrow and gave her a crooked smile, replying, *"You have the wrong country."*

I have never had a personal experience of the above, except for an occasional visit to a few areas where marginalized people lived under deeply saddening conditions. Other than that, I have seen several catastrophic pictures on TV and have had nothing but empathy for such people. The startling part about this incident is that I had never spoken to this woman before except for a few times when we briefly greeted each other. I always paid cordial regards to her. Little did I know she held such condescending thoughts in her mind and even had the gall to express them!

As of this writing, I reflect on such incidents, which were abundant, as a way of God telling me that I need to help these people. The concerning part is that these incidents happened inside and outside the Church. That is to say, people are not even bothered by God being a witness to their wickedness.

During one of our Church services, the Pastor introduced me to a predominantly Caucasian group from North Carolina. He informed them that I was a physician and Medical Director practicing at a clinic in Manhattan. Soon after the service ended, I was approached by a woman.

You will be surprised at what she said to me.

She came up without greeting and said, *"Who gave you that position?"*

I was looking at her face and wondered if she was serious. I kid you not! She was. Well, I cannot recall what I answered then and there, but I do know, for sure, that no human being gave me that position. I have earned it through my obedient response to God's calling coupled with years of hard work, extensive studies, numerous sacrifices, and tears. I know it came from God because He wanted me to restore His broken people, and I took the position because I could not allow such people to fall by the wayside. God's calling was to bless and help lift the fallen through me.

I remember Michelle Obama's saying: *"When they go low, we go high."*

It defines what I have sought to do despite what I have been put through.

It would take another book to mention each of them because there are numerous times when I have experienced that many people often disregard the feelings and presence of others from another race during conversations or other interactions. However, I must tell you that despite all the threats, hate, and adverse actions of folks, God's plan has surpassed and prevailed in my life.

After all, He has encouraged me through His Prophet's words,

"The LORD is close to the brokenhearted and saves those crushed in spirit."

— (Psalms 34:18)

"In addition, the apostle James informs us that we should love our neighbors as ourselves and avoid showing favoritism for the rich over the poor, as mentioned in the following passage "For if a man

wearing a gold ring and fine clothing comes into your assembly, and a poor man in shabby clothing also comes in, and if you pay attention to the one who wears the fine clothing and says, "You sit here in a good place," while you say to the poor man, "You stand over there," or, "Sit down at my feet," have you not then made distinctions among yourselves and become judges with evil thoughts?"

– (James 2:2-4)

I don't think White folks do this to people of their nationality/color, but it seems they have no qualms about hurting the feelings of people of color. It looks as if most of them believe that they have acquired the right to undermine our achievements or bring us down a notch. They think we cannot achieve great things, nor should we be in a place of leadership because of our color.

Don't the above atrocities baffle your mind?

Because of both the experiential and observed indiscretions, I have often hidden from people. I did not let anyone know about my achievements. I would not let anyone come near me other than those who love me; others would have limited access. I never wanted to be in the limelight and performed my job discreetly. However, my Great all-knowing God and guide my faithful friend during high school knew my potential, so He did not want me to become a traditional physician. That is the reason why He sent me to the clinic because He knew I could treat physically and spiritually broken people. Many times, people ask me why I am doing such a low-paying job; I tell them because God has directed me to be there to save the children while practicing medicine for mind, body, and spirit healing.

My calling at the clinic resonates with the situation Jesus experienced during his earthly ministry. In Mathew 4:23-25 Jesus went throughout Galilee, teaching in their synagogues, proclaiming the good news of the kingdom, and healing every disease and sickness among the people. Information about him spread all over Syria, and people brought to him all who were ill with various diseases, those severely suffering pain, having seizures, the demon-possessed, and paralyzed, and he healed them all. Large crowds from Galilee, the Decapolis, Jerusalem, Judea, and the region across Jordan followed him. Similarly, I have been directed to serve at the clinic to treat many young, needy people. I wish I could say that they have all been healed.

"For I know the plans I have for you," declares the LORD, "plans to prosper you and not to harm you, plans to give you hope and a future."

– (Jeremiah 29:11)

The more I analyze and record my journey, the more I realize that I am obligated to draw out and empower our children with courage and boldness regardless of their race, creed, or class. They need to learn to understand and utilize the giftedness with which our Merciful God has endowed them. In addition, I have realized that regardless of our differences, everyone must be willing to share the truth of God's purpose for the unity expected of His diverse and complementary creation.

It is taught in Galatians 6:2 that we have to carry each other's burdens, and in this way, we will fulfill the law of Christ. We are sent to help each other with our complementary diversity. We are made to honor God and His creation.

Folks, young and old, the generations reading this book, please wake up!

Get away from the devil's strategies that lead you to acquire pride. Understand that no one among us is in charge of anyone; we are here to assist each other; the eternal God is in control, and He equips us and supplies all our needs. Children, settle yourself in understanding the words and workings of God, who works miraculously without any time constraints. Strive to understand the magnificent power of the Holy Spirit. As the Bible says, Christ suffered for you and gave you an example of sticking firmly to your belief and obedience. So, follow in his footsteps and learn from the resilience of the excellent standard of Jesus; he stood firm and faithful during the toughest of times.

"Therefore, since Christ suffered in his body, arm yourselves with the same attitude because whoever suffers in the body is done with sin."

– (1 Peter 4:1)

It is my place here to tell you that no man can despise your wisdom and rob your mission. You should never feel threatened or undermined by someone's success. Instead, trust and invest yourself fully in God's calling and assignments, and you, too, will experience success.

This book is free of biases and calls every person to look within themselves and recognize the gifts of God. Throughout my life experiences, I have learned many things, and I want to tell all of you this. Let no one despise your wisdom; let no man rob you of your God-given creativity.

Parents must know that *"It takes a village to raise a child"* is a time-proven quote from an African proverb that shows that it requires an entire community to help the child grow beautifully. In this regard, grandparents play a vital role in children's safety and healthy upbringing. In addition, some studies have shown that children in close relationships with their parents and grandparents are less likely to experience behavioral or emotional problems. This book is prepared by a grandparent who feels obliged to guide her biological and spiritual grandchildren and children.

Given what our society has become coupled with the impact of the pandemic, I encourage you to analyze and utilize your village constituents carefully; choosing wisely will ensure that village constituents are as beneficial as the concept depicts. I testify that if you stay on the right path during these turbulent times, you will see that God has ordained glorified days for you. He is a mountain-moving God who has given you beneficial tools for assistance. He has already selected a team of helpers for you. Ask Him, and you will be given clarity about who your helpers are. This is precisely what the Apostle Paul teaches us in the books of Ephesians and Corinthians.

Knock, and God will open the right doors for you and your children. Teach your children to be careful, observant listeners. Keep the avenues of communication open within your family. God knows what you have been put through and how you have been treated by people who fail to understand His presence.

Such people fall into the devil's strategy and exchange God's truth for a lie. This erroneous belief makes them conclude that they are superior to most of us.

Yet, despite their wrong thinking, believe that our all-knowing and all-seeing God has already opened doors for you that no man can close. God is waiting for you to walk through them. Let's prayerfully help you to find those doors.

Blessings!

Chapter 8: The Miraculous Hand of God

"He who dwells in the shelter of the Most High will abide in the shadow of the Almighty. Therefore, I will say to the LORD, 'My refuge and fortress, my God, whom I trust.' For he will deliver you from the snare of the fowler and the deadly pestilence. He will cover you with his pinions, and under his wings, you will find refuge; his faithfulness is a shield and buckler. So you will not fear the terror of the night, nor the arrow that flies by day ...."

– (Psalm 91:1–16)

The Divine God protects our souls from evil spirits (both inner and outer). He also protects us from negative influences. Therefore, we must strive to follow His directives and calls with vigilance, commitment, and trust. Many who fail to pay attention will find themselves lost and empty. Yet, with the Divine Lord's Grace, we can all breathe and live our lives here on earth to the fullest extent possible; since God puts His miraculous hand over His children for their soul's welfare so that nothing stands in the way of His desire for their happiness and success.

Similarly, I experienced many such protective incidents while working in lower Manhattan. The incidents were so powerful that I felt God's intervention and presence. For example, on one particular day, I was asked by a co-worker to give her a loan of a specific amount. This person was just an acquaintance; I did not know this individual very well except that we worked together. I told her it was not an issue, but I must run this idea through my husband. That is not because he restricted me from spending but because we had many matters on our plate.

Moreover, like all happy and healthy couples, my husband and I always consulted each other before finalizing an issue. When we discussed this matter, we both decided it would be unwise to lend her the amount of money requested because of many circumstances in our lives. I informed her of my decision, which she should have understood. Instead, this incident became the beginning of my woes. I was being set up many times, and one of my co-workers, my friend and prayer partner at the job, alerted me about this lady. She said this woman did not have good intentions for me and that I should be aware of her.

The episodes that followed this particular day were confusing for me. Initially, I could not understand why and what was happening until the Lord began to clear my thoughts and gave me clarity. These events did not necessarily occur in sequence, but the magnitude increased with each passing day. This is because so many incidents were a direct conversation with God to direct me toward His calling. Other times, the circumstances differed, but although hatred and jealousy were present, the Merciful God has always shown and protected me from the personalities of uncaring people.

Most of the time, people base their hatred on jealousy, race, and envy. One of those events that came to my memory was a near-missed accident. I was preparing to go to work and had just descended from the last step of the stairwell when I felt an unexplained push in the direction of our sunken living room. It was a strange feeling because I felt the hand upon me before the angel came.

As I recall, it was not harsh on my back, but it was so firm that it propelled me with a force that I could not stop or stand. My consciousness was fading away, and I vaguely remember crying out to God from deep within, and at the same time, I extended my left hand toward a metallic etagere with glass shelves. It was the only high piece of furniture that was within reach. At that moment, the only thing on my mind was breaking my fall.

Somehow, I stumbled and miraculously fell on my knees just before reaching the etagere. If I had grabbed the etagere, all its metallic frame, glass shelves, and contents would have fallen on me causing severe damage. Instead, after a thankful pause, I got myself together and went to work. If it had happened to someone else, that person might have taken off to clear their mind over the situation. But God has not made me like that; He has given me enough strength to fight back in any circumstance. It was a miraculous event; either the Spirit of God helped me directly, or He sent an angel, but true to His word, He has helped me through numerous situations like this.

On another occasion, while going home from work, I can clearly remember driving Northbound in the right lane of the West Side Highway when I heard an inner prompting to move over. My dear readers, this prompting came at least three times. Still, each time this child of God responded internally with the following excuses: *It's clearing up, the traffic is moving, and it's all right.* I even rationalized the car in the other lane was too close, so I'd have to wait. The car moved ahead, but I still didn't move and was soon given the fright of my life. Finally, the car moved ahead, and I received a quick lesson about the importance of obedience.

For just a few moments after my last rationalization, I felt and heard the largest thud on the roof of my car. It was so loud that I ducked, trying to prevent the top from falling on my head. I was extremely shaken, but since my car was in motion, I continued my journey and safely reached my destination. A day or two afterward, while driving by, I saw a big log that somebody had moved to the side, and I realized that was what hit the car.

God cushioned the blow with His righteous right hand so that it would not cause me any damage. I then understood that His voice had told me to avoid the slow traffic and the impending accident. Since that day, I began asking Him to speak clearly so I could know that He was talking to me and not the enemy. I didn't realize then that the Lord was again speaking, but for some reason, I did not acknowledge Him at that moment.

Otherwise, I would have, like Samuel said, *"Speak, Lord your servant hears"* (1 Samuel 3:10)

From that point onward, I began to recognize His voice. Sometimes He spoke to me through people, and sometimes through His words, my intuition, or symbols. Several of the experiences were quite strange. I have, at times, sat in meetings and felt as if my mouth was muzzled. Answers to questions raised reverberated in my head, but I could not let the answers out of my mouth. As I sat there, I could hear others saying what I was already saying within me.

There was one lady who somehow always found a seat in front of me. I remember she used to wear a broach on her shirt. One day she called in and said she had left something at home and would be late. So she went to her house to get it. Someone close to her told me that this jewelry was a protective charm she wore to overpower people.

I did not believe the validity of that statement, not only because before leaving the agency, I remember her telling me that I was good for this place but more so because of the protective hand of God. My prayer partner and I used to pray together, and the power of the Holy Spirit was quite strong around us. On Tuesdays and Fridays, we would fast so that the presence of God abounded around us.

During that period of my life, many people were praying for me, even the ones I did not know, because the Church directed them to. It was indeed miraculous help from God because the support and prayers of these people helped me continue my journey. They also strengthened me to put out many fires and increased my awareness of godly warnings and directives.

One Sunday after the Church service, the Choir President came to me and said she would like me to be with her and pray for a man. This man shared that he was seeing strange things and was being tormented. Although she was a family friend and a fellow Church member, I told her I had no issues but would only come if my Mom arrived, for she is my prayer supporter, and I needed her there. She agreed, and we entered the room together and saw this man writhing on the bed. He appeared to be experiencing inexpressible pain and agony.

I stood by the foot of the bed and began to pray for his torment. To my surprise, I started praying in the language of heaven, but the Lord kept reminding me that we were in a wrestling match against evil. I could feel the evil Spirit around the room as we were praying. Finally, the evil Spirit started pushing me out of the room. I closed my eyes so that I could see through my spiritual eyes. I cried and spoke in heavenly language tones, and suddenly, the force disappeared. They went away in the name of Jesus. He protected us through His spiritual intervention.

After it stopped, they took this man to the hospital despite my declaration that he needed spiritual intervention, not medical treatment. However, they did not listen to me and took him to the hospital. After a few days, I heard that the medical treatment did not work, and he took his last breath and met His maker.

While these things happened, I scolded myself, thinking I needed to overcome my shyness and fear. However, I later realized there was more to it than *"my shyness."* The enemy was on my back, but when you and I submit ourselves to the Lord God Almighty through His son Jesus Christ, we have an advocate with the Father. We have someone who lights our path, fights our battles, and directs us where we should go.

The Psalmist puts it this way, *"The Lord is my light and my salvation whom shall I fear? The Lord is the strength of my life of whom shall I be afraid."* (Psalm 27:1)

The Lord always protects His children; we only have to follow His path. This is necessary because the enemy is constantly at work to prevent us from declaring God's presence. You and I will meet people whose hearts are empty and whose souls are burdened with a sense of failure. We must tell them that God has not left their side, encouraging them to wake up and look for the signs through which He communicates.

"The Lord will protect him and keep him alive, and he shall be called blessed upon the earth, and do not give him over to the desire of his enemies."

— **(Psalm 41:2)**

I came to learn of his divine protection more pointedly. At work, we were fortunate to be given a lunchroom in the newly furnished facility, which remained our *"healing center"* for several years. We were a close community, so I had no qualms about putting my lunch in the refrigerator at work. However, the incident led me to the hospital, where I was kept for observation. It was indeed the miraculous hand of God that the pain and aches in my abdomen vanished. God had sent an angel to remove whatever my belly was contaminated with. He cleared my body and restored it.

God has communicated with me in several ways and many times. First, I attentively listened to His promptings and directives. If I had ignored them and had not listened carefully, I would have brought death on myself. Then, one day, while in the hospital, He sent a lady to minister to me that He is the healer for all of us. She told me about her husband's terrible crash, but he came out alive. And she told me to trust God through whatever circumstances there might be.

While there, my encounters were not short of miraculous. They were indeed revelatory and awe-inspiring. He constantly showed His presence in my life, which is why I can never turn my back on Him. I know if I did, I would deserve every punishment possible. However, because He is my light and my salvation, and He has given me the grace to share my stories to provide hope so that others can look for His hand, I will do my best to walk in the way He directs and share what He allows.

"This shall be the sign to you from the Lord; For the Lord will do this thing that He has spoken."

– (Isaiah 38:7)

Chapter 9: Abundance in the Most Unlikely Places: More than We Can Imagine

A Song, a Dream, and an Unfathomable Reality

"Now to Him who can do exceedingly abundantly above all that we ask or think according to the power that works in us, to Him be glory in the church by Christ Jesus to all generations, forever and ever." –
(Ephesians 3: 20)

Amen !

It was a tranquil evening, and I was lying in Florida, grappling with information and memories recently uploaded to my mind and spirit.

As a physician and a recently ordained Associate Pastor, I was at a critical crossroads. Crossroads are familiar to me because I have been there many times. I have had to make many crucial decisions at these junctures, both experientially and educationally. I was able to navigate those with ease, but this particular crossroad seems to be an extremely difficult one. I struggled and grappled because I had to make a prompt decision regarding relocation. I call it a crossroads in life because it was at the time of my retirement.

According to my husband, we had verbalized an agreement to relocate to Sunny Florida after securing an early retirement. Still, due to my new God-directed assignment to complete my seminary training, I had become conflicted about the move. In addition, during this period, I had been ordained as an Associate Pastor of the Church, a non-salaried position I felt blessed to have. As a result, my mind was occupied with many concerns, making it challenging to decide.

As any other person would have been, my husband became very concerned about the rapid depletion of our funds to support two locations. He considered this to be an *"unnecessary expenditure."* In addition, he declared that we seem to be deviating from our initial goals. In reflection, I realized that his assessment was correct from a realistic perspective. However, I was reluctant to move in his desired direction since I had repeatedly spoken to God about this specific situation but had not yet clearly heard His answer. For me, His calling was crucial, and I was looking for any directive from God. My husband thought God had spoken, but I was not listening.

In the past, I had frequently received God's specific and timely directives on numerous issues. Those directives were pertinent to my life as well as the lives of others, but for this particular issue, His answer appeared nebulous.

It was difficult because God had shown and directed all my previous decisions, yet this crucial one seemed so distant. As a result, things were becoming increasingly stressful for my husband and me.

My mind was wrapped around the question, *"Why does God appear so silent, or am I not listening?"*

My husband's reaction was valid now that our income level had changed significantly, and we had put a down payment on a new place. In addition to this, I was living in New York. As a result, we both had many things to manage, and we could only live in one place at a time. By then, I realized I must carefully consider my next step before moving.

I was also worried about my husband's disappointment but did not know what to tell him except to apologize. However, I have always waited for God's directives and confirmation before making any major decision, so I decided to rely on Him knowing that it would be unwise to jump to a rapid conclusion that quickly.

Waiting on God Alone

At this point, I was convinced I must be alone with God. Well-meaning voices have spoken, danced, somersaulted, and rumbled with many suggestions, but my inner voice suggested that I rest and have God speak into my spirit.

After much pondering, I was further persuaded to wait on God alone, although those *"seemingly necessary yet interruptive voices"* have often made this resting difficult. For example, my husband wanted to know why I was making a decision that went against our earlier agreement. I wish I could have answered that, but I was waiting for a solid direction. However, that was the only plausible option for me.

As I lay down that night, I planned to actively seek God's directive since a change had to be on the threshold. I began requesting God's commands because I was sure His guidance would come. Although I was still somewhat perplexed, at that moment, I was reminded of God's word penned by the Prophet Jeremiah,

> *"Call upon me, and I will answer you and show you great and mighty things you know not."*

> *- (Jer. 33: 3)*

This verse became my strength and gave me hope in a confused state. Finally, I decided this was the route I needed to take, so I embarked on the journey to communicate with God and again waited, asking Him about His plans.

Looking Back

As I called upon God, many vivid memories of my early childhood were brought to the forefront. The most outstanding ones epitomized the esteem that should be given to older adults for the God-inspiring lessons they have taught. They taught us the value of family, the priority and benefits of sacred space, and, more importantly, the need for total reliance on God, our Father.

My entire childhood reflected God's calling in my life. That was because my grandmother was a spiritual woman who used to receive and follow God's clear directions. Essentially, I was reminded of how she stood up for the Lord.

Granny's Altar/ a Point of Contact with the Dream-Maker

My grandmother gave credence to the importance of the above – her sacred space was established as an altar in the backroom of our family house. I was recently reminded of the significance of having an altar in our residence. At that time, Granny's altar was primarily a table for Godly activities by dear "Granny," as she was fondly called. On that table, she placed her clear water glass and crackers. She used to fast almost daily and would break the fast with the same water and crackers.

We often peeked through a slightly opened door through which we could see her kneeling in prayer and steadfast Bible reading. After which, she would have a cracker and a sip of water from the glass quite late in the evening. She did this in preparation for her ministerial role as an Evangelist, Preacher, and Healer. From this position, God revealed many significant things to her; through these revelations, she could preach and heal many people.

Granny was an itinerant Preacher traveling throughout several parishes teaching and healing. Her work on Earth has benefited numerous people. During our family gatherings, family members have often validated the sacrifices of her calling and the dedication with which she had applied herself over those many years. In the words of my mother, Mildred, Granny's second daughter, we were given the following history.

"Granny" was born in Mile Gully, St. Mary, to Earl and Susan Duncan, a devout couple who ensured their children were brought up in the nurture and admonition of the Lord. Sparks ignited when Granny met Theophilus, a handsome eligible bachelor much like a physical representation of the Biblical Boaz, Ruth's distant relative known then as her redeemer. This bachelor was awesomely blessed because he was one of the largest cattle owners and farmers in Spring Garden, Saint Mary. He was not only a wealthy landowner and farmer, but he was also noted to be a favorite amongst the women in that area.

As a result, many had their eyes on this man, but his heart was set on our sweet Granny, fondly known as dearest. It seemed as if her heart was also placed on him, for they soon became engaged and made plans for marriage, but that's where the similarity ended for before the actualization of their proposed marriage after the birth of two daughters, the first a tall, emotionally strong woman who later became a Preacher and the second, my mother, an ardent prayer warrior. My Granny, the daughter of a God-honoring family, realized that her husband-to-be was not as faithful as expected. As a result, she ended the relationship and immediately returned her engagement ring to him.

Granny began to follow the path of Jesus, the Son of God. She had His miraculous hand on her. First, the Lord would reveal and give her information, then she would pray for the person, and then the individual would be healed. My mom and aunt have shared many stories that I remember pretty vividly. They told us that an evil spirit had overpowered many people in the town to the extent that they were behaving like animals.

They would bark and start doing inhumane things. Finally, somebody came to my grandmother asking for help to heal them. She fasted and asked the Lord to give her directions as to what to do before leaving. My mom and aunt went along with her. As they witnessed the situation, Granny asked my mom and aunt to get water to wash these people and then pray over them.

Mother continued to share in an unrehearsed tone how Granny's decision was solely based on a Godly encounter with the Lord and her subsequent Baptism with the Holy Spirit. This encounter solidified her call to ministry and ignited her spiritual journey. A journey that was initially misunderstood by many and ultimately caused her expulsion from a particular Church that did not believe in the gift of glossolalia or speaking in tongues (Luke 3:16, 1 Corinthians 12:4-12, 27-31 and Acts 1:8) during that season.

Despite the pursuit of her ardent admirer, Theophilus, my maternal grandfather, Granny remained resolute. My mother shared this with me because I had never really known him. He was living in another parish. She moved away from him, declared her absolute commitment to God, and, like Biblical Abraham, stepped out into the unknown world. By reviewing her life's activities and her impact on her community, I was open to the fact that God would use anyone who willingly obeys Him. He would also be found by anyone searching for Him with their whole heart.

Our family has been blessed with revelations and direction. For example, my mother took my sister and me on a road trip. Though I do not recall the exact reason for our trip, there was a meeting at the Church.

One lady came out to my mom, and we met her before entering the building.

She told Mom, *"One of your children will become like your mother."*

At that moment, it did not hit me. Only after I reflected on the matter did I realize what she meant.

Before that, I used to think it was my sister, and I often said to her, *"What are you waiting for? Why don't you move forward and start manifesting?"*

After a while, I started receiving the spiritual gift of discernment and manifested it for everyone's betterment.

I cannot recall the exact date and day I began to get dreams or say things that would turn into reality. However, it was surprising and somewhat exciting when my dreams started coming to me.

My Granny was abundantly blessed with spirituality.

Each time I heard a story about her healing and guiding someone, I would be reminded of the verse by the Prophet Isaiah 55:6-7: *"Seek ye the Lord while he may be found; call ye upon him while he is near. Let the wicked forsake his way, and the unrighteous man his thoughts: and let him return unto the Lord, and he will have mercy upon him; and to our God, for he will abundantly pardon."*

She would always seek the Lord first before doing anything. Similarly, I started seeking Him during my studies and encouraged others to seek Him as they worked hard. I would only go for formal Biblical schooling once the Lord laid His hand heavily upon me. I prayed and called out to Him for directions. The direction used to be specific; He would plan the path, reveal it, and I would take the next step.

He guided me like He guided my grandmother. I was directed to leave things He would not allow. I occasionally went to the club on special occasions. They were nothing like today's clubs. Those neighborhood clubs were safe community gatherings where people danced and had fun around shared interests such as dominoes, volleyball, tennis, and other sports. There wouldn't be any despicable behavior. I went a few times when I was younger but sometimes felt guilty, especially about dancing, because our Pastor hinted that dancing was wrong, so I stopped going. Similarly, the Lord had directed my grandmother not to marry her fiancé.

I remember, once, my cousin asked me to go with her to a New Year's Eve party. I liked celebrating with family, but I went with her. I never knew it was in a club where older men sat by the counter waiting to be served. I wanted to leave immediately because I knew this place was not for me.

So, I told her, *"I need to leave. My spirit was uncomfortable."*

From that point onward, I embedded myself in my studies and Church. I started attending youth group meetings and anything that would keep me focused because I knew the Lord was preparing me for more incredible things. So many people say it is conscience, but I believe it is God's Spirit alerting us on our paths.

I remember my earring fell in the lake; it was a gift from my husband.

I recall committing the situation to God, *"If you help me find this, I will commit to you forever."*

So I asked my daughter to pick it up. She went under the water and found the earring at the bottom of the lake. I kept that earring a symbol of my commitment for a long time. I do not know where it is now, but I remember not wearing it often because I feared losing it.

He has showered me with mercy because I was unharmed, even by things that should have harmed me. He protected me through His grace and put an overarching umbrella over me.

By all of this, I do not mean I am perfect because I only try. I get angry like everyone else but try not to make negative remarks. I remember one time I invited people to my house for an event out of the goodness of my heart. When they left, my husband

and I found out that someone had taken an envelope with our emergency money from the office area in our home. I was so upset that I wanted to lose control of my tongue. My husband reminded me of my promise to the Lord. He would say leave the vengeance to the Lord and remember you have children. My husband truly is a God-sent help. God used a physical being first to alert me, thus enabling me to experience the Holy Spirit's power.

Proverbs 16:1 further asserts, *"The preparations of the heart in man, and the answer of the tongue is from the LORD."*

As a result, although hurt and angry, I held my tongue and deferred judgment to the Lord.

Granny responded to the Lord's promptings and was immediately drawn to His will and way. Her obedience preceded a very excellent chapter of her life. A chapter that held and expressed great significance for others as God manifested His workings through her life. Workings, which I can only term God's will.

Chapter 10: Granny's God Orchestrated Acts: The Deliverance of the Demon-Possessed

My mother, her sisters, and other neighbors have testified about many unusual God-orchestrated events. As mentioned in the previous chapter, one such incident occurred in Mile Gully, where Granny was born to a Christian couple, Earl and Susan Duncan. Her childhood home was nestled within the low-lying hills of the parish of St. Mary, Jamaica. It was a town of lush greenery, undulating hills, and valleys where the sun would peak brightly over the mountains, its rays glistening over a seemingly lazy river with its hidden, silent depths.

Granny often journeyed from this area to Highgate, a town that was a few short miles from her home. Highgate was viewed then as a commercial hub since it housed the post office, police station, market, and central bank of the district. A few members of Granny's family used to be midwives in the local area. Several of her grandchildren have been trained and worked in the medical field, affirming God's gifts of healing assignments in our family.

As the Bible describes the story of the Levitical Tribe, we can see that Amram's sons were Aaron and Moses. Of the two, Aaron was chosen for a particular work. He and his descendants were selected and assigned to be the only ones to do this excellent work—to prepare the Holy things for the Temple service. They were the ones to burn the incense before the Lord, to serve Him as Priests, and give blessings to the people in His name forever. Looking back, I see where Granny's lineage has been endowed with the gifts of healing enablement – critical individuals in her lineage are chosen to do specific medical work by God's directives.

One day while returning home from one of her Highgate trips, Granny was approached by a neighbor who frantically told her that her help was needed because many people in the district behaved as if they had become bewitched. The neighbor relayed that the people seemed to be under some spell, exhibiting animal-like behavior, barking, howling, and hooting. I do not know how Granny felt, but I heard and noted that Granny's heart of compassion leaped into action.

Granny hurried home and prepared to help. She prepared by heeding **Matthew 6:33**, *"Seek ye first the kingdom of God and his righteousness and all other things will be added unto you."* She first sought the Lord's counsel, affirming that her actions were God-directed. Then, as instructed by the Holy Spirit, she, in turn, directed my mother and her two sisters to fetch as many buckets of water as possible.

I can imagine the eager but trepid anticipation with which they went back and forth to the river. Their young hearts must have throbbed with excitement as they hurried up the hills, over the stones, and around the corners to fill those water drums. So they did their part, and Granny did hers.

Granny fasted, prayed, quoted scriptures, and, as told by our elders, physically washed the demon-possessed as directed by the Holy Spirit. This process was repeated day in and day out, and after several days by God's grace, the people returned to their normal state. They had not eaten for several days, and so dear Granny and her family cooked and fed everyone, and the people all returned to their respective homes clothed in their right minds.

Granny was walking in the footsteps of Jesus, for as mentioned in **Luke chapter 8,** *"We see where Jesus commanded those present to feed the twelve-year-old girl – the daughter of the ruler of the synagogue after he conducted her restorative healing."*

During my early childhood, I became exposed to several other miraculous moments as Granny allowed herself to be used by God Almighty, the only true potentate. One such moment is indelibly imprinted on my mind. The gist of the event is as follows. Some of my siblings were home when Granny informed my Mom that two policemen were coming to see her, and their intentions were not good.

Granny expressed this very calmly. She did not appear to be afraid. Granny used God's blessing to help people, and her conduct allowed the Holy Spirit to flow through her to heal many. She continued to do so even while she was living with us. After she did her pastoral work, going through parishes, preaching the word, and conducting healing, she returned to live with us.

Soon after her declaration, the two policemen arrived and promptly stated the reason for their presence. They informed her that they had come to arrest her because of a report that she was committing abnormal spiritual acts. Granny responded with what can only be described as the revelation of knowledge – a God-given spiritual gift. The police officers were strangers, but she looked at them compassionately as she told them separately about the information known only by each individual.

First, she declared that one policeman's wife was sick with abdominal pain and vomiting. She then explained that a woman with whom one of the men was involved had caused his wife's illness. The officer began to cry. She then turned to his associate and disclosed another significant piece of information.

They then, in awe, turned to Granny, saying, "You are a Prophet of God, for only He could have revealed those things to you. So you are safe with us."

With or without the police officer's affirmation, my grandmother would have continued on her assigned mission as she was only working unto the Lord.

It is analogous to **Daniel 6:12-28** *"When the king wanted to destroy Daniel by throwing him into the lions' den. But, when he heard Daniels's voice the following day, he declared that Daniel's God was the God of Gods, the Lord of kings, and the revealer of mysteries. In other words, He is the true and living God."*

Similarly, the policemen said that Granny's God is the living God. This prophetic gift was manifested in another way. It happened somewhere in the late '50s when Granny shared prophetically that a chair was explicitly turned down in the White House. She continued to say that the chair would remain in that position because it was awaiting the appointment of a Black President. Then and only then would it be turned right side up for only he could sit in it. It became an eye-opener for me when in 2008, Mrs. Clinton and Mr. Obama were both vying to be the Democratic nominee for the Presidency of the good old U.S.A.

A robust debate ensued as our family gathered in our usual stomping ground, the kitchen. One of my very vocal sisters was adamant that Hilary Clinton would rise as the chosen candidate because it was time for a woman to sit in the Presidential suite.

Then and there, Granny's words lit up, and I firmly responded, *"No, she won't win, look at how Barack Obama came on the scene. His ascension is God's blessing."*

This man was virtually unknown to most, yet look what he accomplished. He is the Black man whom Granny prophetically mentioned becoming President. The rest is history, for Mr. Obama did win the election.

The above incident and many others were not foreign to us because they occurred within our physical space. A space that was then our home. Although it seemed that help was forthcoming primarily to and for strangers, many healings and deliverances were also lifesaving and germane to several of our family members.

One such family deliverance began on one of those warm sultry summer days familiar to the people of Jamaica. A day when children were frolicking playfully in their yards under sunlit skies, a day when my second youngest sister went to play with a friend in another small house in the complex: As was the custom, she left her sandals at the door and went inside to play. They were so absorbed in childhood pranks that they were oblivious to the fleeting time.

The setting sun and the hunger pangs that would signal the hour for their evening meal had unknowingly approached. It was only in response to my mother's call that my tenderhearted sister donned her sandals and skipped hurriedly home. But undisclosed to her and the family, the enemy had already stepped in.

I am uncertain about the time of the unfavorable change, but the difference was prominent and noticeable for my little sister. I was not much older, but the nature of the situation, considering its repetition at family gatherings, has left me with a poignant memory. The picture of my baby sister's profuse itching is etched on our minds. Tender loving care and regular prayers were comforting but did not stop the itching.

Moreover, the medical doctors could not identify the cause. Finally, one-pointedly advised my mother to seek spiritual help. Granny's giftedness was the help needed, but she was off on a mission trip to the parishes and could not be reached. Telegrams were sent to her last known location, but still, she could not be found. Mother waited prayerfully, and then our faithful grandmother returned. Rosie was covered in rashes over her skin, and Granny's work on her was supernatural. She returned and took the child to her home, and after praying and fasting, she did what the Lord directed. The results were astounding.

My sister, who had been discolored due to a constant pruritic rash and had stopped eating, bordering on anorexia and death, was restored to health. She began eating soon after Granny completed the cleansing and deliverance process revealed by God. It was indeed an act of faith and empowerment as the demonic presence left Rosie's body.

"This is the confidence that we have in him, that, if we ask anything according to his will, he hears us: And if we know that he hears us, whatsoever we ask, we know that we have the petitions that we desired of him."

-(1 John 5:14-15)

My Granny, an elder of the Church, had proven herself as a woman called, appointed, and anointed by God. Our beloved Granny prayed over Rosie, dipped her seven times in a shallow hole in the ground then anointed her with oil in the name of the Lord Jesus Christ. That act reminded me of Naaman's cleansing, and in the latter years, it has helped to strengthen my faith in Jehovah Rapha, the Lord God, our healer.

Mother and Granny, elders of the Church of the living God, asked in confidence, and our God, the true and living God, heard and helped them as they responded to James 5:14 with a question, *"Is any sick among you?"* Then as directed in verse 14b, she prayed over little Rosie, laid hands on her, and anointed her with oil in the name of Jesus.

In addition to her gift of healing, Granny was a Preacher, Prophetess, and prayer warrior. She worked with God's words. It affirmed to me that God's words contain power. I hope others find encouragement from what she did and how she used God's words to heal people. This will help them heal themselves and strengthen their belief and faith. I am writing this book because it is my prayer that just as God's words have encouraged me, they will also inspire you, the reader.

The life and acts of our grandmother affirm what I have come to realize, namely, that the gifts and callings of God are genuine without repentance. They have no distinctions as to race, class, color, gender, or creed. More importantly, during the tenure of His earthly ministry, as Christ lay dying on Calvary's cross and through His resurrection power, Jesus elevated and restored all people, including women, to the place He had first appointed them. His word declares that before He placed each of us in our mother's womb, He had already knitted every detail of our life – mind, body, and spirit so that we would accomplish the task for which He was placing us on this earth.

Granny performed many other God-orchestrated deeds that will be relayed later, but I must move on to first discern the lessons that are being sent from my dear Granny's experience.

The first lesson is that a sacred space is an absolute necessity if I or any other person is to understand and accomplish the purpose for which God has created, protected, and kept us on this earth. The sacred space in the house is a place where we can talk to Him and hear Him without any interruptions. God directed me to help and heal the children as I did this in my home. I have also started doing this isolation practice in my office. God meets us when we carve out that unique place and invite the spirit in.

The second lesson is to honor or at least understand the role of others who have physically and spiritually impacted our lives. For example, my dear Aunt Mamma, the last of Granny's daughters, greatly influenced my life. She was my mother's youngest sibling. In the early years, she lived near most of us, and in the latter years, she lived with one of my siblings in what may be considered a God-given family house. Her down-to-earth, gentle caring manner has been a blessing in disguise for all children in the family, many for whom she has been a caring, protective babysitter. Her love for us was so strong that our pain and joy became hers.

She was one of those loving aunts who would step into the place of our dear mother whenever necessary. Her closeness has allowed us to give her the endearing name *"Aunt Mamma."*

Like her mother, she believed and acted according to Jesus's words, *"Suffer the little children and forbid them not to come unto me, for of such is the kingdom of heaven."* (Matthew 19:14)

The third lesson was from my father, who provided the necessary instructions. He provided for his large family by working two jobs until my mom could work outside the home. He was a pharmacist's assistant. The first practical lesson he gave me as a teenager was instructions for bodily care. At approximately twelve years of age, my Father brought me a care package with deodorant, my very own soap, and perfume. I was thrilled. Instructions, however, do not always come only through gift-giving and pleasant events.

On one occasion, he incorrectly judged a situation during which he assumed we were up to no good because he found a neighbor, a young man, in our house. Without asking any questions, he slapped me firmly. He did not know I had already determined I would not let anyone mess up my life. He was not privy to that information. The sting of that slap and the misjudgment immediately emphasized the importance of intercommunication. I was, therefore, more determined to prove him wrong.

The fourth lesson was when I was just under seven years of age, and my eldest sister, under the Holy Spirit's guidance, noticed my passion for reading. Therefore, she took me under her wing and strengthened that ability by providing the tools and methods needed. During the summer holidays, she would take me to the parish of Saint Mary. There in that vibrant, healthy green district, she introduced me to older folks who would sit under shady green trees or in rocking chairs on their verandahs, listening keenly as I read stories from the books I carried around. Their enthusiastic and intuitive participation was one of the fuels that strengthened my zest for reading.

My family is loving and supportive; everyone helps each other, the older ones helping the younger ones and the younger ones helping the older ones develop newer skills. My grandmother had started this path, and we all took up the mantle and ran with it.

This love for reading continued, and I embarked on a detail-oriented journey through books. A trip that unveiled a door to the unknown and the intricacies of the human body. An immediate love connection ignited a more profound passion for learning more— the details I had to discover. To me, they were like priceless treasures hidden in a field. I was ready to give my all to find this treasure.

As I can recall, my sister's nursing manuals were the first significant human anatomy fields available for exploration. They provided terrific insights; pictures of the various organs were so fascinating that I could not pull away. I believe it was during my late childhood that I could often be found locked away in the house's single toilet stall, lost in a book, and oblivious to the world around me. You can well imagine the frustration of those who wanted to get in. As I matured, I found other reading niches, such as the library, while traveling on buses and trains, you name it.

I did not realize it then, but looking back, I can see where God began preparatory work in my life.

While playing around the house, I often draped my sister's stethoscope around my neck and pranced around singing, "*I'm leaving on a jet plane. I don't know when I'll be back again.*"

It was indeed a prophetic utterance of a future that awaited me. During another instance of our childhood frolicking, one of my sisters began to express what I later learned as the classical signs of choking; her hands were at her throat, her eyes were bulging, and she barely whimpered. I do not know precisely why I did this, but no adults were around, so I slapped her in the back a couple of times, and out of her mouth popped a guinea seed (pit), and soon after that slap, she was again her usual playful self.

I was intuitively wired to perform choking first aid and, later, the Heimlich maneuver. But, when my eldest sister, my mentor, left for a nursing program in Macclesfield, England, my passion for the medical field became stronger. It ignited a flame when I visited the Kingston Public Downtown Hospital.

I cannot quite recall the reason for my visit, but I can clearly remember seeing a young male doctor in his below-the-knee white coat with a stethoscope and a writing pad in his pocket. He was giving someone health-related directives. I was so fascinated that my eyes and ears were affixed to this picture. Then and there, the last flicker of my seven-year-old fascination with the intricacies of the human body became a true passion. As a result, my desire for medicine and my love for becoming a doctor immediately solidified. Moreover, that wish became a built-in un-coerced goal, for when my dearly beloved grandmother became ill, I often rushed home from school to prop her up and help her however I could.

Unfortunately, that help was often only to offer a sip of water when possible. I watched her as she lost her appetite, weight, and strength. I observed the change in her color, her intolerance for food, and her inability to care for herself. During those times, I vowed to find the cure for whatever was ailing her, which I later realized was cancer. Seeing Granny sick, a woman who healed so many for so long, was saddening.

Time rolled on, and I did not deviate from that goal. But in tandem with that desire, the power of the Holy Spirit was cultivating another love in my heart.

Although He was wooing me toward Him, I had nothing to do with this; it was all God's doing.

James, the Just, the brother of Jesus, says it this way: *"Listen, my dearly loved brethren. Has not God chosen those whom the world regards as poor to be rich in faith and heirs of the Kingdom that He has promised to those that love Him?"* (James 2:5)

I am the fifth of eight children born to diligent and hard-working parents. We lived in a clean, warm, comfortable house with a shiny verandah, a small front yard, and a relatively large backyard. My grandmother raised pigeons while not traveling as an itinerant Preacher and Evangelist; we also had ducks, chickens, and a puppy. The dog became my guardian angel.

We were comfortable and safe in a loving family who believed in the importance of faith, family values, and education. Unfortunately, there were many people who, from a distance, felt that we probably had too much and were envious of us. Nevertheless, I applied my God-given ability and my passion for learning and was rewarded with a fully paid scholarship to high school.

As a result, someone whose daughter did not get a scholarship threatened my life and vowed they would make me pay. They tried, but as I look back, I can only thank God for His grace and mercy and for alerting my family members. Mother and other loved ones were praying for me, and God sent me a dog which became my protector. She followed me to school every day. Although the children tried to chase her away, she would wait for me at a distance out of their reach.

Then to my painful surprise, one bright sunny morning, as I opened the French doors to the verandah, the puppy rushed ahead of me, brushing against my legs. I was horrified to watch her spin around and drop dead before me. My elders declared that she had taken a blow meant for me. The word of God clearly states that when God is for you, no one can be against you, and I am incredibly grateful for his protective hand.

The Apostle Paul in 1 **Corinthians 1:27 says,** *"God chose things the world considers foolish to shame those who think they are wise. And he chose powerless things to shame those who are powerful."*

In reflection, I can confirm with the Prophet Isaiah, as Isaiah 54 verse 17 recorded, *"Those weapons will form, and tongues will rise against us in judgment. Still, it is the heritage of the servant of the Lord God Almighty to condemn every one of them."*

Friends, I was only a child then, but I was guided by loving spiritual women – my mother, aunt, the eldest sister, a loving grandmother, and a dedicated, caring father. These individuals are treasures that I hopefully have not taken for granted. These people individually and collectively ensured that I was exposed to the things of Christ, and they, therefore, fostered within me a love for God. They also nurtured the hidden gifts that were buried within. These are things that every child deserves, but not many receive. Some have said it takes a village to raise a child. This proverb has sparked many debates. Many have rebutted the statement that it takes a family to raise a child.

However, I will declare that it takes a village, meaning an equipped caring society and a family, to raise a child. But, the development of a successful child takes more than that. Raising a healthy, successful, and productive child requires Godly intervention and guidance.

I believe the words which are my family's mantra: *"Train up a child in the way he should grow, and when he is old, he will not depart from it."* (Proverbs 22:6)

My youthful years were truly God-directed. It is near midnight, and I vividly remember many late nights of earlier years as I sat at our dining table delving into my books, analyzing every necessary detail. I could see and occasionally hear my mother in the background as I pondered the questions. She was washing, cleaning, and ironing, yet watching over me, prayerfully accompanying me as I studied.

I owe her a debt, which I can never truly repay except to be ever grateful to God for placing me in her care. I have watched her as she reflected the love of Christ by caring for her family and community. I have watched as she sacrificed time, talent, energy, food, resources, and income so that the needs of others could be met. I have observed her as she expressed love during trying circumstances and forgave and guided us through that process following scripture.

During those years, I did not fully understand. I might have even taken much of it for granted, but it became more apparent and straightforward each day and was even more poignant during her illness. As I'm recording my experiences, one of my God-given messages, *"The ministry of motherhood,"* came to mind.

In retrospect, I can only attribute this message to God's guidance and the manifestation of His love through the instrumental support He has allowed from the lives of counselors such as my dear mother.

The standard definition of the word ministry has been described as *"the work or vocation of a Minister of religion, a Pastor, Evangelist, Missionary or a Christian conference speaker."* However, based on scripture and the work of Jesus, that of Mary, His mother, Esther, Dorcas, Paul, Peter, Daniel, and a host of others, a more Holistic concept of ministry should be considered. The definition serves a worthwhile purpose from the dictionary's perspective, but I would like to consider a mild revision.

For my purpose and from my exposure, I believe the word *"ministry"* should be seen as the faithful service of God's people rendered unto God and others on His behalf. Historians have recorded the sayings of many famous men who have attributed their success to the faithful service of Godly moms and grandmas. In 1 Timothy 5, the apostle Paul described Lois and Eunice as women of genuine faith. This type of faith was restricted not only to those women but also to their sons and grandson.

A significant part of Timothy's success as one of the Apostle Paul's longest-working associates must be attributed to his mother, Eunice. This commendation is affirmed by the apostle Paul, who credited her as the person responsible for Timothy's faith. We can only conclude that Paul saw it necessary to honor him and his mother because his mother took the time to apply the true principles of Godly motherhood to her son in his formative years (2 Timothy 3: 14-15).

There he encourages Timothy with the following words:

"But as for you, continue what you have learned and firmly believe. You know those who taught you, and you know that from infancy you have known the sacred

Scriptures which are able to give you wisdom for salvation through faith in Christ Jesus."

- (2 Timothy 3: 14-15)

Like Paul, I would like to honor my dear mother. Mother was part of a women's group. In addition to the weekly Church services, we experienced weekly prayer and Bible study as these women came to our home for weekly meetings. As a result, I would like to point out three things my mother taught me that all Godly mothers should teach the children God has put in their care. My prayer is that every mother will follow these three examples.

In caring for their children, my mother and many before her reflected and modeled the ministry of motherhood as they exemplified complete reliance on God and His principles. As a result, we were never hungry, were never left unwashed, and were always nurtured and loved. But as these practical things were done, we were also being gently washed with the water of the word. These principles' knowledge and consistent application will help Christian moms see a much-needed change and improvement in the next generation.

Consistency in prayer, the first principle, comes from a picturesque view of Eunice, the mother of Timothy. In Acts 16:1, Eunice is described as a Jewish woman who became a believer. Being Jewish, we can conclude that Eunice – the victor -as her name implies, was schooled in scripture and the observance of many prayers offered to God there in her home and worship center. The book of Proverbs clearly states that mothers and fathers should train their children in a specific way. However, He also said children should act in a God-directed God-given manner. Eunice committed herself to prayer. She also meditated and sought guidance through prayer. She encouraged and enhanced Timothy's giftedness with these as part of her arsenal.

The second thing that caught my attention, and hopefully will grab yours as well, is that Eunice of Scripture and my dear mother became living examples of the word. Eunice taught Timothy, and my mother taught my siblings and me the truth and wisdom of scripture.

Mothers, no single thing will significantly impact your child more than the truth of God's words, the scriptures. You can read all the parenting books about fun, food, and fitness for your child; plan thrilling birthday parties and top-notch arts and crafts projects, but none can outdo the teaching of scripture. I encourage you to teach per your child's developmental abilities and desires. So, reading, music, and dance help children move in an upward and forward direction by teaching scripture.

These women also lived out the truth in the presence of their children. They did not lie to their children. They tried to be as honest as possible; they did not say anything and did another. As a result, their children developed a genuine love and desire for scripture. I can genuinely say that my mom passed on love from and for the scriptures. That aspect of her ministry to my sibling and I has contributed to God's Evangelistic mission in and through our lives.

A vivid story comes to the forefront, and that's my mother's caring or self-effacing character.

My family and I were returning from an event. Unfortunately, I was not in a joyful place, and I allowed my anger to be expressed unforgettably. We were getting into our customized traveling van when I slammed the front door in anger without checking.

To my embarrassment, my dear momma's fingertip was severed, and instead of responding in anger, she declared, *"I'm glad that it's not one of the children, for they could not bear this."*

I was embarrassed and distraught. But, for me, it was and continues to be a lesson in humility.

Thirdly, when husbands were unavailable to teach Biblical truth, Eunice and Momma enlisted Grandmas and God-fearing men. The mother-grandmother team worked collectively and positively for the common good of their children and grandchildren.

The success of these teams affirms and recommends that grandmothers should not be overbearing or controlling, but they should willingly and graciously provide loving support and prayers.

In *"The Gift of Grand-parenting,"* Eric Wiggen, a sage, remarked that older people should slow down and stoop over to see things as children do once again. By stooping over, they can hold the hands of children who toddle along on inexperienced feet. Things such as the bug on the sidewalk, the snail under the cabbage leaf, the robin pulling the worm from the rain-moistened earth, and the blinking, bobbing snowman are things small children and their grandparents notice and enjoy together.

"Children's children are a crown to the aged...."

-(Proverbs 17:6)

I was blessed with a godly mother, a grandmother, and a hard-working father: I feel particularly blessed to have them all. I say I have because although they are now physically in heaven, their memory and lessons continue to live on. They are a part of the cloud of witnesses who still cheer me on. The apostle Paul was one of Timothy's God-fearing men and mentors. So as I continue preparing this guidebook for my children, I am thrilled to say I am now the happy grandmother of a group of seven adorable biological grandchildren and many more spiritual grans.

When God created man, He clearly stated that it was not good for man to dwell alone, so He created a partner. That partner, the woman, was made with specificity. God ensured that she was suitable and complimentary for that man. He then blessed them and directed the two to become one; he led them to multiply and fill the earth. They were each made with a body that would complement an oppositely designed body in accomplishing this purpose. Read the Genesis account with an open mind for the revelation of God's truth. He wants us all to be happy. True happiness is experienced as we walk in the proper light. He desires to bless each of His created beings so we can find the path back to Him.

Reflecting on my family dynamics, I recall my Father working diligently at two jobs to provide for his family. Despite his long hours, I recognize that he took the time to ensure we were adequately clothed and fed. I remember his fatherly tenderness when he saw the change in my development - my transition from childhood to young adulthood. He handled this in a way that I will never forget. Upon his arrival home, his children occasionally saw a small paper bag containing goodies for the tummy in his hand.

On one particular day, he unexpectedly brought home a much-appreciated care package of deodorants, perfumed soaps, etc. He had noticed the change in my development and spontaneously acted. I can also recall the importance of my mother's presence in keeping my balance, especially when he was away. As a result, I have always been protective of my parent's relationship. I thank God they have remained together throughout their lives and ours, thereby modeling the importance of marriage as a Godly lifelong commitment.

As a family, we have been introduced early to the word of God and Bible studies. My family would have meetings where they taught Bible lessons and memory verses. I would sit in their discussions and listen to them. The Lord had been schooling me since my childhood through my family. These teachings even allowed my father to be a devoted, supportive man who cared for his family. Several family members have left this world physically, but I am sure they are around me spiritually.

One time, I remember everyone was telling me to go to Florida for a vacation. Standing beside the closet in the hallway, I looked at my mother as she mumbled softly. The thought of *"nothing lasts forever"* rushed through my mind. The Lord was giving me signals. As I went on the trip, Mom got sick. I told my sister to take her to a particular hospital, but she took her to another one. I should have stayed with Mom in the hospital, but I felt I had to take my sister back home.

That was the night my mother's condition went downhill. It still bothers me today because I sometimes wonder if I had made the right decision.

I believe people in the hospital were responsible for her worsening health because I saw many young doctors who did not even wash their hands and did not put gloves on while handling her. Perhaps, she got an infection. I still think about why I did not stay there afterward. Maybe I could have intervened. Why did I not speak up? It was hard for me to survive for a year because the magnitude of pain was touching the sky.

My mother needed doctors committed to helping her and others in a caring manner, but this type of commitment is severely lacking in our society. Our community is being instructed to view many things in an ungodly way. For example, marriage is now considered something totally unlike that which God Almighty intended. It is unfortunate and often painful to see because our society is in a place of disobedience. It is spiraling to a place where we, as humanity, will truly reap the rewards of our investments.

The Bible states that parents suck sour grapes, and children's teeth are set on edge. Parents ought to take that warning seriously. In Genesis, The Book of Beginnings, on the sixth day of the creation period, God commanded man, saying, *"Be fruitful and multiply; fill the earth and subdue it; have dominion over the fish of the sea, over the birds of the air, and over every living thing that moves on the earth,"* **(Genesis 1:28)**

Through obedience to God's command and the birth of children to a one-man and one-woman commitment, God's Creation Mandate would be fulfilled. Moreover, that Mandate was neither retracted by the fall of Adam and Eve nor by the flood because God re-stated it in more detail, as seen in Genesis 9:1-10. By God's standard, marriage should thus remain a covenant between the husband, wife, and God.

Research shows that, on average, at least two children must be born to each family to maintain the population at its current numbers. Thus, *"to be fruitful and multiply,"* each family should have two or three children. Since God's work is primarily through His people, the argument could be made that Christians should have *"many"* children. ***"For they are a "heritage" and the "fruit of the womb and his reward."*** **(Psalm 127:3).** Expansion of families may also occur through the adoption of children. For a healthy family and societal existence, these children should be given the full rights and responsibilities of *"naturally"* born siblings.

Yes, a primary benefit of marriage is not procreation but companionship and wholeness.

"And the Lord God said, it is not good that man should be alone; I will make him a helper comparable to him."

- **(Genesis 2:18)**

While the remainder of the creation was *"good,"* even *"very good,"* God declared that it was *"not good"* for either man or woman to be alone. In addition, He stated that both need a *"helper"* to complete what the other individual lacks in their abilities. Therefore, God intended marriage for a lifetime.

Ephesians 5:31 clearly instructs, *"Man shall leave his mother and Father and hold fast to his wife, and the two shall become one flesh."*

We should note that children are present for only a part of that time, but families are still expected to fulfill the Creation Mandate of fruitfulness. They can accomplish this by working as grandparents and mentors, even after their children have formed their own families. This fruitfulness can also be performed as they pass on their wisdom to community members.

The Bible is clear that teachings on saving faith are to be passed from one generation to the next (Deuteronomy 6:1-9; Acts 2:39; Ephesians 6:4). In the Old Testament, explicit responsibilities of the covenant (land, laws, Levitical priesthood, etc.) were passed on in this way. So likewise, God's primary mode of Evangelism is through the family name from generation to generation.

With the disruption of families and the erroneous teachings in many families and societies, the primary mode of continuity and expansion of truth is missing in our postmodern culture. As a result, children are often self-taught or guided by manufactured rules and or through the devil's influence. Haven't you observed the fallout from this?

At this point, I would like to ask you and me to ponder three questions:

1. **Are you and I praying consistently?**

2. **Are we living examples of God's word?**

3. **Are single moms and dads enlisting Godly parental support from Godly mentors of the opposite sex?**

If we aren't, it's time to develop that sacred space where The Lord can communicate with us. I endeavor to do that more consistently so that God can share with me for the rest of my journey on this earth. Doing so will honor His name and allow me to be a living example of God's word and a blessing to others. **Are you willing to join me?** Please do it will be beneficial for you and our extended family.

Chapter 11: Life in America: The 2nd Leg of My God-Directed Journey

When I think about the fifty years of obedience, dedication, and loving sacrifices made by the Bronx Baptist Ministry, and my family, I genuinely thank God for our Pastor and other members who have helped me on that part of my journey. God promised and described Himself as our Helper (**Deut. 33: 26; Psalm 46:1; Isa. 41:10-14; Hosea 13:8**). God helps us at all moments, especially when we cannot help ourselves.

My visit to the United States fulfilled prophetic words, which the Holy Spirit allowed me to hear as a child many years before as I cheerfully did my chores in our Myers Street house in Jamaica. When I sang, I'm leaving on a jet plane; I had no idea that those words—a dream in song—would become my reality. Yet it did because I did leave my country on a jet plane in April 1969, and I now fondly remember my first days in America and the Bronx Baptist Ministry with much love. This ministry began in a neighborhood house called the Honeywell Baptist Church.

Several years before leaving Jamaica, I can also vividly recall a visit with my mom and my second-youngest sister to Upper St. Andrew. There we met a woman with the spirit of discernment. This woman, whom I had never seen before, looked directly at us and told my mom that one of us standing there would become a healer like our grandmother. Of course, I immediately assumed that it was my sister, and from that moment on, that statement was relegated to the far recesses of my mind.

Nevertheless, several years after that pronouncement, I left on a jet plane for the trip of a lifetime and whatever that journey had in store.

It all began in the spring of 1969, when, upon leaving my home in Jamaica and the Jones Town Baptist Church with a letter of transfer in hand and specific advice to seek out Pastor Simpson, a previous member of that Church, I landed at John F. Kennedy International Airport and was picked up by two ardent members of Honeywell Baptist Church.

Honeywell Baptist Church was then a blossoming ministry under the leadership of its founder, the Reverend Dr. Samuel G. Simpson, his wife, Mrs. Lola Simpson, and a small team of ardent believers.

During the early weeks, I sat as a keen observer and saw and experienced the warm expressions of love and unity as I listened to the unadulterated word of God. I knew then, without a doubt, that this was my new Church home. Honeywell's membership soon outgrew the small house Church building. Upon the ministry's relocation to its current site, I quickly became involved in the expanding Friday night Youth Group meetings. Those meetings afforded the youth numerous fun-filled, rewarding evenings of exciting debates, interactive discussions, and stimulating presentations under the guidance of competent youth leaders. At that time, youth group members in our church remained until they were just below the ripe young age of twenty-one years of age.

I was already in college, and I was committed to this. A short time later, I quietly began my career training in medical school. That journey was quite an eye-opener. It was astounding and slightly intimidating since I was part of a minority in a predominantly Jewish setting. Some professors quickly told us we had a specific artificial place, not the God-directed place of excellence to which God himself had assigned us, but my reliance on God brought me through.

My God-given giftedness and my pre-ordained high school preparation in Jamaica were beneficial catalysts for my studies in America. Because of these, I graduated with a Cum Laude Bachelor of Science in Chemistry from Hunter College and a medical degree from Downstate Medical College. While on those two legs of my educational journey, I rarely, if ever, missed any Church-related meetings.

After graduation, several members secretly approached each other with the following statement:

"I had no idea she was in medical school. When and how did she do this?"

While working part-time to help offset my college-related expenses, I met a young man who became one of my most ardent admirers. I often ignored his invitations and gifts, but this did not deter his pursuit. Finally, in one of the rarely spoken responses that I go to Church, this very handsome young man readily offered to attend a Church service with me. The rest is history. He later became a diligent attendee, my husband, and a member of the Bronx Baptist Church.

We married while I was in college and were blessed with three children—one at a critical stage of my educational journey. People are often surprised to know that nothing seemed extremely difficult even while I was going through it. It was chiefly because I was on my God-ordained, God-directed journey. I have often jokingly asked my husband if he had done something to control my mind, for I can clearly remember that when he asked me to marry him, I felt as if I were under a cloud and was moving in a dream-like state when I accepted his engagement ring and his offer for an impending marriage.

Over the years, I have seen that our marriage was all a part of God's plan for the journey of our lives. The mighty and eternal God's power foiled the many external physical and demonic attempts to sabotage my studies, work, and life.

"The Lord directs the steps of the Godly. He delights in every detail of their lives. Though they stumble, they will never fall, for the Lord holds them by the hand."

(Psalm 37:23-24)

The following experiences affirm His protective, delivering presence. I first recall being scheduled for a Physics and Calculus Exam on my college campus on a cold and blustery morning. However, my supportive husband requested that I deliver a crucial document to a Manhattan location near my College campus. The commute, however, was more complex than I thought, and so after completing the task, I was stranded as there was no bus in sight, and not a single taxi responded to my signals.

I ran, I walked, and while bracing against powerful winds, I arrived at my destination. Upon entering the classroom, I noticed everyone silently seated as if glued to their examination papers. After softly apologizing to the teacher who handed me my test paper, I became numb because my mind could not gather around the thoughts. It was as if I had yet to study. I went blank for what seemed like an eternity, but I quickly cried out to God for help at a crucial moment.

It was not too late, for I began to recall the material I had studied for the test. It was clear that the Holy Spirit came to me—he settled my anxiety and aided my memory, just as God had promised in His word.

God, who had begun a good work in me, was performing what he had promised *(Philippians 1:6)*. I'm not sure how much of that truth I understood then, but I became calm, and my eyes were certainly opened to the Holy Spirit's assistance with my test and the enthusiasm for God's truth.

After leaving the youth group, a ministry in which many of us developed long-lasting relationships, I became a member and subsequent leader of the Gospel Vibrators ministry, which began in the early 1980s under the leadership of Sister Monica and subsequently under Brother Orville. My leadership skills were honed in this young adult ministry, and my spiritual growth sharpened. Following Matthew chapter 25, this group visited and ministered to those in prisons, namely Spofford Juvenile Detention Center, Rikers Island, Otisville, and the Bedford Hills Women's Center.

As a group, we also encouraged and attended to children in group homes, parks, and on the highways and byways of life. Through its discipleship program, the Gospel Vibrators ministry also facilitated life-enhancing skills, leadership building, gift identification, warm fellowship, friendship Evangelism, and enhanced worship.

Although most members were not professional singers, many heartwarming, spirit-led songs have been performed under the leadership of gifted musicians such as Grace Barton, Sydney Brown, and Roy Jennings. Video graphics and vibrant concert memories were captured at home and as we traveled.

In walking down memory lane, I can recall many spiritual landmarks, such as the excellent choir and other choral performances that have displayed the rich singing legacy and gospel messages from our Senior Choir, Combined Youth Choir, and praise ensemble, as well as the vibrant Sunday evening training union meetings and other community events. These all bring back very warm memories. However, I can also vividly remember the Biblical messages, lessons, and prophetic words that have strengthened me and affirmed my calling.

On a particular Sunday after one of our regular services, I had just recessed with the choir and was standing at the back of the inner sanctuary when I heard the following words: *"Neglect, not the gift that was given to you by prophecy with the laying on of the hands of the presbytery"* (1 Timothy 4:14). At that moment, I had no idea of the Biblical location of the verse, but I knew that I was being spoken to. I heard it clearly in my spirit.

I was directed toward a more profound Biblical truth and a deeper, genuine encounter with God through the Holy Spirit, but I remained hesitant. So I continued to encourage others, both practically and spiritually. Many people appear to find their path, as I did, or so I thought. As some went on to seminary, I continued to pursue the medical way until God intervened.

Isaiah 55:8 records, *"For my thoughts are not your thoughts. Nor are your ways my ways, declares the Lord."*

It took a while for me to realize this. But as I reflected on my life journey, God's directive became more apparent through the guidance of the Holy Spirit. I had accepted and committed myself to the Lord at twelve, but I did not understand the Holy Spirit's role, presence, and power until He revealed Himself to me. Only after studying the work and ministry of the Holy Spirit were my eyes fully opened to His call.

Many people have argued about who He is for centuries. For all of us, the question to be clarified is, therefore, *"Who or what the Holy Spirit is?"* Is he a person, a force, a power, or an inanimate object? During this phase, I came to know Him as a person from my studies, chiefly because the word of God declares Him to be so, but also because of His ministry in my life and His role in my family's legacy, as manifested earlier in my grandmother's giftedness and Godly interactions and activities; my mother's prayer power; and the dedicated lives of others.

I was also challenged to know the truth about Him because, in one of our young adult meetings, we were told that the Holy Spirit's role was drawing the unsaved to Christ and other specifics, such as speaking in tongues, were not for today. Upon hearing that statement, my heart sank, and I became saddened because it brought to the forefront the question of the reliability of my dear grandmother's walk and actions. I heard and saw her works, and if they were not of God under the guidance of the Holy Spirit, we were all in trouble with God and were, of all men, the most miserable.

Therefore, I continued to seek God's truth avidly, and he led me to a detailed study of the Holy Spirit's personhood, role, and deity. This study gave me knowledge, wisdom, understanding, and the baptism and fullness of the Holy Spirit.

I have learned that when we ask, seek, and knock, God will not only allow us to find what we need, but He will also give us what He intends for us to have for His honor, glory, and blessings. One of my earliest recollections of my Holy Spirit encounters occurred when I committed to praying for someone sick. A plethora of other encounters have amply demonstrated His identity and mission.

One thing is sure: God's declarations and revelations are always specific; they are sometimes somewhat unbelievable yet fascinating. Over the years, this experience has drawn many of my immediate family members and acquaintances to Christ.

Historical records confirm Spirit-filled retreats, mission trips, and weekend getaways to Pennsylvania farms and its *"good and plenty"* and other restaurants where we have had a bountiful supply of fresh air, organic fruit, vegetables, meat, and other farm-raised animal products, but more importantly, ongoing clarity on God the Father, God the Son, and the Holy Spirit. These retreats' peaceful, spiritual atmosphere has been where divine and prophetic truths have come to light.

As I currently continue to experience and participate in ministry under the new leadership structure and its cadre of God-appointed supportive men and women directed by our current capable under-shepherd, Rev. Frank I. Williams, I am thankful for my earlier training, and I'm very excited about the evolving future prepared by God before the foundation of the world.

Due to the supernatural power and ability of the Holy Spirit, I can encourage us to stay on the right path with God. We should never forget that every prayer said, every child dedicated, every marriage performed, every home blessed, and every visit made are spiritual landmarks that will continue to do what God wants them to do, which is to build relationships, strengthen our faith, and bring glory to God.

Therefore, my sons, my daughters, my grandchildren, and all spiritual children, as the journey continues, *remain strong in the grace, mercy, and peace that are available from God the Father and Christ Jesus our Lord (2 Timothy 2:1)* through the power and presence of the Holy Spirit, and your joy will be complete.

Chapter 12: Healing Aids

"Nevertheless, I will bring health and healing to it; I will heal my people and let them enjoy abundant peace and security. Although we know that complete physical healing may not occur in this lifetime, we also know that God has a plan and a purpose for our lives."

- Jeremiah 33:6

Indeed, God allows suffering and healing. We have all gone through the horrific COVID-19 epidemic, and many may be wondering what will happen during the upcoming seasons when viruses and bacteria tend to multiply and thrive. But, as I reflected, strength came through the words of Joel, which says, *"I will restore to you the years that the swarming locust has eaten, the hopper, the destroyer, and the cutter, my great army which I sent amongst you." - Joel 2:25*

During the horrific COVID-19 season, doctors, researchers, and their assistants have avidly worked to create a vaccine, and their dedicated expertise continues to be appreciated. Like many others, I hoped this development would occur sooner rather than later. It eventually did, but while waiting through increased infections and unprecedented deaths, I pondered what the average individual and, more so, I was expected to do as a medical professional. During that time, I was reminded that God sends locusts as trials, troubles, and tests into our lives, but I thought maybe now was the time to believe they had pierced us long enough and it was now time for restoration after all God has promised to restore that which the locust has eaten. However, the question was *how*.

As I pondered the question, I was reminded that with wisdom, our forefathers had documented through practical experience the benefits of several natural products. Some were used to eliminate coughing spells, many to heal wounds, and others to stop bleeding. With a closer look at the benefits of these products, many of us have realized that combining such products has been beneficial in reducing the impact of many infectious agents, including the coronavirus.

The answer was revealed to me after the Spirit of God directed me to analyze the components of these natural products.

A reminder of their use was first shared when The Holy Spirit sent a woman who had declared her firsthand encounter with them. He later confirmed the reasons for the beneficial impact of each ingredient through a dream in which He awakened me in the early hours of the morning and prompted me to research the benefits of four specific elements. I immediately did, and this research has proven beneficial to many.

The combination given and proven most beneficial includes ginger, garlic, and lemon blended in apple cider vinegar and water. First of all, ginger and lemon are highly immunogenic. This means that both items contain ingredients known to stimulate leukocyte production. The production of this cell line is crucial because leukocytes are designed to fight infections.

These ingredients also have significant fighting power against free radicals. For example, Vitamin C in lemon and ginger is a potent antioxidant. As a result, it is highly effective in eradicating free radicals, which are destructive agents against the body's normal functioning cells. In addition, garlic is highly immunogenic and anti-inflammatory, meaning it has the power to clear up bacterial and viral infections.

What I came to realize is that garlic is also antithrombotic. It also reduces oxidative stress and is known to detoxify heavy metals in the body. Doing so reduces the negative impact of free radical toxicity on blood vessels, blood pressure, and cell membranes.

From the above Godly revelations, I realized that people were dying not from pneumonia as initially presumed but from micro clots in the body. This revelation came to me in April 2020 after the death of a very supportive member of our Church family and during an intense prayer vigil offered up because of my daughter's severe COVID-19 symptoms, along with the suffering the virus was causing many across the globe.

After that revelation, medical research showed that the COVID-19 virus was causing clotting in the body, confirming what the Lord had previously revealed. Namely, micro clots create blockages known as thrombi and the resultant destruction of the body's organs. That, my children, and not pneumonia, was one of the main reasons many fell prey to the virus's deadly impact. God is indeed a revealer of secrets.

The Book of Proverbs 2:6 says, "The Lord gives wisdom, and from His mouth comes knowledge and understanding." So likewise, in Psalm 18:15, the psalmist declares, "The heart of the discerning acquires knowledge, for the ears of the wise seek it out."

Children, the above verses clearly say that God is the one who gives wisdom to those who seek it. As a result, we must listen to Him because it comes from His favor and blessing. I, therefore, implore you all to develop both a heart and an ear for knowledge.

The severity of COVID-19 and the Holy Spirit's intervention obligates me to record the most effective natural remedy chiefly because its proven health benefits were experienced and expressed by users.

So with the divine wisdom of our Creator and His plan to restore that which the locust has eaten, prepare at your discretion and with your doctor's advice.

- 8ozs. Braggs apple cider vinegar
- 1/2 pound ginger
- one head of garlic
- three lemons
- 16 ounces of water

Blend all ingredients, then boil for a maximum of five minutes. (Do not over-boil, as this will destroy beneficial nutrients). Other individuals have added turmeric powder and preferentially utilized various combinations of the above.

After preparing, take one teaspoon three times daily if sick. For prevention, take one to two teaspoons daily as a preventative measure. Store the rest in a glass bottle in the refrigerator.

In addition, continue to practice these safety guidelines recommended by the CDC. Good health and blessings to all. Above all, remember that God has provided herbs (natural products) to heal deadly diseases. He has given us the wisdom to understand the properties and benefits of these natural remedies.

Reflecting on how I came to obtain and analyze the recipe mentioned above, which I now realize and share as an inhibitor of the COVID-19 virus, I am truly grateful for God's guidance and timely encounters. I am uncertain of what came first, but I remember being called by one of my Church members who provided information on a remedy that had worked against COVID-19.

I immediately questioned her on how she knew about the mixture's effectiveness. To which she said, *"Don't worry. I know this because it has kept several individuals out of the hospital."*

Soon afterward, the Spirit of God directed me to analyze the benefits of several natural products. Many of these were among the items our elders in Jamaica used and recommended. I can clearly remember my mom and grandmother using several of these to help many individuals, including their children.

So, I hopped out of bed with eager anticipation. I grabbed my phone and searched the web to see why God had chosen these natural products to help His children. As I began my research, I was pleasantly surprised and gratefully educated on the benefits of the items recorded in the recipe above.

In addition, upon looking back, I recall being called to offer the intercessory prayer during a specific Sunday morning worship service several years before the dreaded resurgence of the COVID-19 infection.

As I prayed, I walked down the center aisle, declaring that God had provided us with all we needed to heal people worldwide. This alert was, therefore, not a total surprise because that prayer was said many years before the virus returned with an even more life-threatening variant. However, I am also shocked because, during my early years working with the homeless population, God had clearly instructed me to practice *"Mind, Body, Spirit Medicine,"* or what I have since called *"Holistic Health Care."*

As I record these experiences, I pray for God's guidance and the ability to listen to Him more avidly. I am sure that in this period, He has directed me to follow His precise orders to restore my husband's health, and I am grateful for that. My husband, the one He has given me, is a blessing. But, unfortunately, it would take another manuscript to tell people about our journey together.

I honestly could not accomplish half the things I have without him. *"To God be the glory"* (**Galatians 1:5**). Jesus said the following to His disciples in the gospel of Mark, *"**What therefore God has joined together, let no man put asunder**" (Mark 10:9)*. It seems that many have tried to do so but praise God for His wisdom, His keeping power, and the spirit of obedience He has deposited within us.

As I sat here trying to decide what to record next, I prayed, reached out to God, and was reminded of several loving memories. But, before documenting those memories, I must have us focus on an event. My youngest sister's text came through at two o clock on

Monday, December 14, just a few minutes before it was needed for me to remain faithful to God's nature; when He wants to guide me on a particular path, He sends alerts through various avenues. This one came to me in preparation for my youngest son's two-sixteen afternoon request.

Fourteen minutes after her text, he reported that his baby's mother had just received a frightening medical report. Her physician had informed her that an ultrasound revealed an abnormal nuchal translucency measurement in her first trimester of pregnancy. Such a report often suggests a congenital chromosomal disability and possible retardation of babies delivered to older women. The doctors recommended abortion, given the possibility of her delivering a disabled child. However, although we were a bit tentative, we prayerfully accepted God's gift of this new life regardless of the possibility of a potential disability. As a result, by God's grace and favor, our grandson was born without complications and is one of our happiest grandchildren.

My sister's text was informative as it affirms the value of every life. While looking for a part-time lunch replacement, her text shared that a supervisor found that her only hope was hiring a developmentally disabled young man. At the interview, she shared that although his appearance and speech shouted his diagnosis, his outlook and excitement for life were undeniable. Therefore, she said she hired him for reasons known only to God.

Unfortunately, the rest of the staff were informed of his special needs and were unhappy. They told her how they felt about working with someone differently abled. But he had already been offered the job and was onboard to run the grill three hours a day for three weeks.

A fantastic lesson was learned then and continues to be relevant today: the new young employee became an asset rather than a liability to the company. He could not multitask, but he had a photographic memory. Back then, in that store, there were no computers. The cashier had to call in the orders. After only three days, every sandwich maker wanted to work with the young man. He became a great asset because he remembered the smallest detail of every order.

Business improved as he expedited the service and lightened their workload. He was later accepted by those who initially rejected him and was often found on site long after his working hours, providing historical data unknown by others. He was a walking, talking calendar, as per the supervisor. His mother was delighted to know he had finally found a place of acceptance.

Folks, within our world, there are many like that

young man. We are all a little like him, so with each encounter, let's try our best to accept each other.

James 1:17 tells us, *"That every gift is from God."*

We all have different talents and God-given gifts, but they are all important and can be used for God's kingdom.

Healing can occur in so many different ways. Encouragement is one of those ways that is often overlooked. I was recently directed to the hospital to remove something present for almost ten years. Upon arrival at the hospital, my husband and I encountered a woman who shared that our encounter was a miracle for her.

As she shared, I realized that the Holy Spirit's presence was palpable. She mentioned feeling frail and disillusioned and was ready to log out for the day. Her feelings were so strong that she told the volunteer working alongside her to attend to the next patient on her list. However, as she walked by us, she was prompted to stay longer.

As it turned out, I was the next in line to enter the pre-surgical suite and was called by her. She mentioned that she felt praise bubbling up in her, and we began to talk about the goodness of God. She later shared that her weakness resulted from rare bone cancer, but despite her diagnosis, she felt compelled to work to share the love of God and the path back to

Him with those who were broken in body and spirit.

I was immediately prompted to pray for her strength and her healing. After our encounter, she explained that she no longer needed to leave as she had received strength and courage for the day's journey. I, too, was encouraged to continue my journey. On the following day, at the end of my procedure, several staff members came in to introduce themselves.

Among them was a young lady who introduced herself as *"just a Tech."*

Listening to the disparaging way she expressed herself, I couldn't help but say, *"You are not just a Tech. You are a Tech placed in that position by God, who made you and has assigned you for such a time as this."*

Remember you are fearfully and wonderfully made for a purpose; this is a stepping stone for the more important things God has in store for you. Before she left, I told her I would like to speak with her later. God arranged our follow-up encounter in preparation for my discharge; I had to walk around the hallway to ensure my balance and respirations were good. As we walked, I began to share some miraculous things that the Lord had done in my life. I continued asking her if she believed in God and had accepted Jesus as her Savior. She answered in the affirmative. I further told her about the gift of tongues and how the Lord had affirmed that His gifts and callings are irrevocable.

Then, she said, *"I know why I had to come to work today. I didn't want to, but the Spirit of God kept telling me to go. I had to hear from you."*

With a changed demeanor, she expressed that she was about to cry but was thankful for our encounter. Children of God, remember that encouragement is vital for optimal health.

Our spoken words of encouragement can bring healing. It restores both body and soul, as mentioned above. The word of God tells us, *"The generous soul will prosper, and he who refreshes others will be refreshed."*

–(Proverbs 11:25)

Therefore, plan to be generous healers.

Chapter 13: Loving Memories

"Now may the God of hope fill you with all joy and peace in believing, that you may abound in hope by the power of the Holy Spirit."

– (Romans 15:13)

As we grow and look back on our tears and sorrows, they often make us laugh, but I'm sure many never knew until later that past waves of laughter could also bring tears. Memories are astonishing in that way. We often only realize the value of an experience as our life progresses, and the experience becomes a memory. So, children, be aware that such occasions and experiences will bring many beautiful but sometimes harsh moments into your lives. Therefore, always cherish and thoroughly evaluate the present moments because they become memories, and memories stay forever with you and your loved ones.

What are my loving memories?

One such memory is a reflection of the caring heart of my mom. My mom could have been here in the United States between 1964 and 1966, but her mom, my dear Granny, was not well. She was very ill, so when her brother, a math professor in New Jersey, offered to sponsor her, she told him that the timing was off and she could not leave their mother since he couldn't leave his job in the United States.

As a result, he sent for her youngest sister, my beloved aunt. Mom remained in Jamaica and cared for Granny until she died in 1966. Granny's homegoing service was terrific. I am unaware of precisely why this happened – it must have been because of her excellent deeds – preaching, healing, caring for the sick, and participating in the deliverance of many, coupled with the difficulties of telegraphic message transmission. She had served her purpose in life just as God had planned for her. She was blessed by our gracious God and the thankfulness from many who needed her. For days after her death, busloads of people were still coming to her funeral, which was already over. It showed how many hearts she had touched in her life.

For me, my mom was a person who stood in the gap for others. This was evidenced by the way she treated other people. It must have been a family trait acquired and passed down through the generations. Like Granny and Mom, my sisters and I have received this gift of accepting God's calling with the ability to express a self-sacrificing nature. I remember my mom giving up her meals to the neighbors. I've watched her design clothing for the naked, and just like Granny, she sheltered the homeless.

She was raised to care and a helping hand, a principle she passed on to us. My mom made innumerable efforts for the Lord, just like my Granny; she ministered, healed, and participated in the acts of God's deliverance for many people. Hence, I am passing this down to all children and the upcoming generations through this book. I want the younger ones to see that caring for others is possible because of Christ's love and grace.

While in High school, I often remember her sacrifices as she watched over me, silently accompanying me as I studied. In addition, she made sure that all her children were given the tools to find their way to God. This is one thing she never compromised. She has taught us many lessons, but the one she prioritized is that everyone deserves to be loved and cared for. My mom taught us to love everyone regardless of any reservations.

The Bible mentions this teaching in *John 15:12-13*, *"My command is this: Love each other as I have loved you. Greater love has no one than this: to lay down one's life for one's friends."*

My mom has been gifted with immense patience and tolerance for pain. The Bible says in *Proverbs 31:25*, *"She is clothed with strength and dignity; she can laugh at the days to come."*

Stating the core memories of my life will only be complete if I discuss my childhood memories in my beautiful home. My mom and dad showed great taste when choosing and styling our home. Our home was designed for eight children.

Unlike what many people of other persuasions have falsely concluded and have even insinuated, we lived in a lovely five-bedroom house with a verandah that encircled a large living room that ended up by the door of a small bedroom that could double as a library or office.

Our living room had three entrances; one was a prominent French door that opened onto the verandah facing the street, and to its right was another small door that was rarely used. And as the patio arched to the left, another door was in the middle of the wall. From this door, we could walk across the verandah down some steps into the yard at the side.

Two gardens were on either side of the steps facing the longer rectangular wall. I can recall an enormous Gungu tree and cane and tomato plants in one; in the other were flowers of various types.

Finally, toward the back of the house was a rectangular room used as our dining room. Mom would be in the kitchen while I would do my homework. She would constantly come and check on me and ask if I needed help. I used to think she was busy in the kitchen, but in reality, she was keeping an eye on me so that I could complete my school assignments on time. We could directly access the kitchen, a large bathroom, and an independent toilet room (my reading retreat hideaway) from the dining room, all under one roof. This physical space with a loving, caring family provided peace.

The description of my home should answer many people's concerns over how my race has been living. A lady a few years back wrongly pointed out how I might be living miserably, that is, in a horrible condition, because this is a stereotype she and many people live by. This needs to stop right now. We have had many successful figures and many more to come. They have achieved many great things in life, just like any other race has done.

However, given our complexion, many assume this gives them the right to underestimate our value, history, capabilities, and feelings. People immediately think that we are from backward areas when they see our skin color. I am often puzzled by the ones who make these accusations or have these innuendos. It is so exhausting and so trite. I used to be taken off guard, but now I'm so busy seeking to grow deeper in the deliverances directed by God and to use my talents for His honor and glory that I'm prayerfully trying to use such remarks as teaching moments. The sad thing is that this view is entrenched despite the talents and successes of many individuals with varying complexions and complexities.

I know that God said, *"Let us make mankind meaning human beings in our image and likeness. And let them have dominion over everything else."* (Genesis 1:26-27)

I also know that such negative responses are levied because of sin-unbelief in God and unfaithfulness to Him and His words. Nevertheless, the repetition is quite infuriating and, at times, extremely painful. I have had so many experiences over the last fifty-one years that I intend to ensure that the upcoming generations will see their value a n d maximize God's giftedness and values.

By doing so, I anticipate that they will thus rise above the innuendos and live as God intends. *After All, they are fearfully and wonderfully made* (Psalm 139:14). I also anticipate that they will realize that with God on their side, they are spiritually and positionally *placed as the head and not the tail, above and not beneath, as expressed in Deuteronomy 28:13.*

Another memory of my mom is the essence of her compassion and her God-given tolerance for pain. As mentioned earlier, one particular evening, we were getting in our family van. It was a custom-made vehicle for trips which my husband had bought. I believe I was in the early part of one of my pregnancies. I was upset about something negatively impacting my emotions, leading my mom through tremendous physical pain.

Many believers today do not acknowledge true spirituality because they have a dull affection for Christ. This can only be eradicated by remembering all the blessings and being grateful for what God has done for you and me through Jesus Christ. That memory of God's great act keeps our focus in the right place and the fire of love burning for Christ.

I have seen many youths caught up in worldly issues. They either do not know or do not remind themselves of the great price that Jesus Christ paid for us. The Bible has repeatedly reminded us that unbelievers are drenched in sin and cannot identify the enemies of God. There is no doubt that Satan and the haters of God have blinded them.

However, God never leaves His searchers in vain. He is graceful and merciful and lets His perfect Son die on our behalf. He sets an example by doing so much for us – he did something we could not. He gave His only son, who sacrificed His life, to pay the price needed to satisfy the judgment required for our sins. He has also promised never to leave or forsake those who are His. Reader, please make sure you give yourself to Him. So that, in times when Satan tries to disconnect you from your Lord, the True and Living God, you will be protected.

I want you to remember these words: *"Fear thou not; for I am with thee: be not dismayed; for I am thy God: I will strengthen thee; yea, I will help thee; yea, I will uphold thee with the right hand of my righteousness."* (Isaiah 41:10 KJV)

Lessons learned on the evening of Mom's trauma have helped me hold my tongue on many occasions as I remember and reflect on the following passage, *"Refrain from anger, and forsake wrath. Fret not yourself; it tends only to evil"* (Psalm 37:8).

My anger caused my mother unnecessary pain. Yet, from that pain, I could see her then and continue to see her in a different light—an illuminating light of compassion, love, and strength. I have learned throughout my life experience that we all become nothing but a memory at some point. So to speak, my children, make sure you become a good memory for others. A good memory will be a lasting and beneficial legacy.

As I complete this portion of my memoir, I encourage each of God's beautifully designed people to keep the meaning of the passages mentioned close to their hearts. For in them are numerous lessons to be extracted. These lessons are treasures that will help you and your family understand the reason for your existence, the reason you are placed in a particular family at a specific place and time.

Above all, they will help you see the mountains designed for you to climb, the heights only you can conquer, the friendships you must forge, the many victories validated for you *to win*, and a world for you to change by God's grace.

My Children/my readers,

After documenting this segment on loving memories experienced from my interactions with my family, I realize there are many other miraculous experiences I cannot record now. I ardently hope to share those at a later date. Until then, I trust that *you will continue to grow in wisdom, stature, and favor with God and man. (Luke 2:52)*

Love and Blessings to you all.

Amen!

Made in the USA
Columbia, SC
21 September 2023

23155259R00104